SOURDOUGH

SCHOOLMARM

The Letters of

MARION CAMPBELL GREGERSON

Marion Campbell Gregerson

Edited by

C. DONALD CHRYSLER

SOURDOUGH SCHOOLMARM

Library of Congress Catalog Card Number: 92-90425
ISBN 0-9633908-1-3

Cover courtesy:
Solvay Animal Health, Inc.
Mendota Heights, Minn.

Chrysler Books
Box 243
Marne, MI 49435

DEDICATION

To our *Sourdough Schoolmarm*,
Marion, and her beloved family.

CREDITS

Editors ... Merle, Gearldean and Arthur Chrysler

Computer Printing .... Victor Sifton

Poetry .... Blanch C. Niewiadomski

Chapter Divisions

Chapter   Page

YUKON QUEEN

When I was only twenty,
I dreamed someday to be
The queen of all Alaska,
With her gold meant all for me.

When I was one and twenty,
I sailed the mighty sea,
On the ship *S.S. Victoria*,
A Yukon queen to be.

From Nome I went by dog sled,
'Cross miles and miles of snow,
To become a lady teacher,
And the prize of ev'ry beau.

In Council I was candied,
And pampered left and right;
The importance of my mission
Brought my kingdom close in sight.

I donned my reindeer leggins,
Mukluks and parka neat,
To become a royal vision
And a queen you couldn't beat.

With the smell of seal and tomcod,
And the wolf howl at the door,
I learned that Yukon royalty
Had lots of work in store.

When I was two and twenty,
I signed for one more stretch;
My labors seemed so small
Beside the king I meant to catch.

The ice had thrice left Niukluk,
The sun had blued the sea;
Alaskan queen and sourdough
Were now the same to me.

I had my king, my mansion,
And life was hard but full;
With school, and love and drudg'ry,
I learned how huskies pull.

The sleds that we saw racing
Across the frozen land,
Gave cause for celebration,
Proved the tie of dog and man.

When I was four and twenty,
Alaska shared my tears,
As I learned that cruel lesson-
No help when danger nears.

The hard life of Alaska
Became the life for me;
While I taught them their letters,
What a wealth was brought to me.

When I was seven and twenty,
Her snow, her life, her fears,
Made me love this Alaska,
Taught me wisdom beyond years.

I did not see my crowning,
Nor rule a royal band,
But learned through passing seasons
Just to love God's frozen land.

Blanch C. Niewiadomski

PREFACE

SOURDOUGH SCHOOLMARM

The Alaskan scene is changing so rapidly that the days of the sourdough, tomcod and mukluk are all but forgotten. These letters, the first of which was written over fifty years ago, were miraculously preserved down through the years to give us today an eyewitness report of what old Alaska was really like.

In 1920 Marion Campbell, a young midwestern girl, accepted a position as school teacher in the village of Council, Alaska. She signed for one year and stayed eighteen. During those years in Alaska she wrote many letters to her family and unintentionally captured a portrait of a culture now fast fading away.

As you read you will meet Marion's sisters Helen, Jessie and Margaret, and her young brother Leonard. You will sympathize with Tom, the boy she left behind, and smile as she relates her adventures as the only single girl in an area populated with lonely miners, sailors and traders.

This is the story of a young girl's hopes, fears, delights and disappointments. It is a story of adventure, romance, tragedy and success--relived now in the letters of a *SOURDOUGH SCHOOLMARM.*

Chapter I

Alaska Bound

At twenty years of age Marion was beginning to tire of her routine as a teacher in suburban Chicago. One day as she perused the INSTRUCTOR magazine, she noted a full page advertisement requesting teachers for the territorial schools in Alaska. Why not? she asked herself. An adventurous young lady, she responded eagerly and, far sooner than she thought possible, found herself on the way to Seattle, Nome and finally, the little village of Council, Alaska.

Somewhere in Minnesota
September 16, 1920

Dear Folks,

I hardly know how to begin this letter because of the surprises in store for you. I am on my way to Seattle now and from there I go to Council, Alaska (near Nome) to teach school. I will be gone ten months. I am sorry I could not let you know sooner or come home, but the call came very unexpectedly Monday night and I left Chicago last night. The notice was so short I did not have time to say goodbye to anyone, not even the next door neighbors. I just packed my trunk, gathered up a little money, said goodbye to Jessie and Tom, and left!

I am to get $1,800 for nine months in a little school of one room and eleven pupils. The town has about 80 people, just a small place, but very near the port of Nome, in the heart of the seal fisheries. I expect to come home next summer with a sealskin coat . The temperature at Council is about zero at this time of year but as the climate is dry, the cold is not noticeable. At least that is what they keep telling me. But you have no need to worry; Tom is doing enough for everybody. The poor boy is almost heartbroken that I am leaving him behind.

I arrive in Seattle Saturday night at nine-thirty and leave on the steamer *S.S. Victoria* Sunday morning at ten o'clock. We are passing through the most beautiful country just now, hills so high on one side you can't see the top from the train and a beautiful river on the other. I have just gotten up and have not eaten breakfast yet. I have an upper berth and am travelling in a tourist car which is cheaper than a standard pullman.

We are to arrive in St. Paul at ten-thirty this morning. Don't you think I am the luckiest girl there ever was? This is going to be the most wonderful trip for me and an adventure that I have longed for.

I have had so much excitement that I have hardly eaten anything for the past two days and am getting hungry now so am going to eat some lunch. You should see my luggage - a suitcase, travelling bag, two magazines, two boxes of candy, a box of lunch and my purse.

I am wondering what river we are following and wishing I had a map. It is the largest river I have ever seen and must be half a mile wide. It does not look so very deep but has a rocky shore and we are within ten feet of the water. Just now there is an opening in the cliff on the other side and it looks as though another river flows into it. I am right and the river is much narrower now. I just overheard someone say that the large river is the Mississippi and the one coming into it is the St. Croix. Well, so much for the rivers.

Now don't worry about me for Alaska is not nearly as bad a country as is generally supposed (perhaps I can even pick up a few gold mines). I will be under government protection and the doctor will keep track of me through several big Chicago companies up there.

I never dreamed of going to the Coast so soon!

I must say goodbye now but will write more tomorrow.

Love, from Marion

Seattle, Washington
September 21, 1920

Dear Folks,

I have not left Seattle as yet but shall leave on Thursday. The *Victoria* sails Thursday at ten a.m. I told Jessie when I wired that I would not go but I am going on after all. The trip over the mountains made me sick and I was very discouraged when I arrived in Seattle.

But the few days of rest have put me on my feet and I am going after all. I would have missed the *Victoria* because of being ill but the sailing was delayed because of a bad storm. Do you suppose that means I really am supposed to go?

My new superintendent is here in Seattle and took me to lunch today at one of the finest restaurants called, of all things, the Pig'n Whistle. He gave me the details about my work and I know I shall like it. I am to teach in a one room school and will have no janitor work to do. From what he tells me, I will be a big frog in a little puddle.

Mail is delivered in Council once a week so I will receive letters all right. And I will surely appreciate them. I am all enthusiasm now except for one thing. I hate so to tell Tom that I have changed my mind again and am going on after all.

My trip over the mountains was a wonderful experience. We passed Glacier Park and crossed the Rockies at night but all day Saturday we were in the Cascades. They are beautiful and the Columbia River and its valley are indescribable. For the first time in my life I have seen snow in summer. We passed through numerous tunnels and over many trestles. I am enjoying western fruit to the fullest extent, both seeing and eating. The Washington apple orchards are a grand sight. Every little valley in the Cascades has its apple trees. Peaches were killed here last year but the pears, prunes and grapes are delicious.

Seattle is a watery town. It's on the sound, spread out for miles and has three lakes (one almost twelve miles long) and it rains continually. The sun shines on one house while the next is drenched with rain. Some hills in Seattle are so steep that I feel I must sit down and slide. And yet they park cars on those steep hills just like on level ground. People here seem so slow. I can walk circles around them.

So many exciting things to see! They have some of the old-time cable cars here. A cable runs under the ground between the two tracks, something on the order of a derby racer. Streets are crooked here because of the hills and there are no amusement parks. Quite a change from Chicago.

Well, when next you hear from me I will be wearing reindeer leggings, hood and cape - a regular Eskimo. I am already learning many lessons in geography.

By the time you get this I will be on my way - seasick perhaps, but you may still wish me good luck and bon voyage.

Lovingly, Marion

Somewhere in the Bering Sea
October 2, 1920

Dear Family,

Just about three more days and I'll be through travelling. I will be so glad. Have been on the water for ten days now. We stopped in Ladysmith, British Columbia for about thirty-six hours which of course delayed us for awhile. We expect to arrive in Nome tomorrow night or Monday morning. After that I will have only two more days of travel. We have had quite rough weather and all the ladies have been seasick except me. Of course there is time yet; I have almost slipped a couple of times but not quite. I am notorious all over the boat because I was the only woman able to go to the dining room for several days and the only woman on deck most of the trip. This old boat surely does roll and pitch. The second night on the ocean was terribly rough. My stateroom partner was so sick I didn't go to bed at all but lay on a lounge all night. The lounge was about two feet longer than I and I kept sliding along it with every roll of the boat. There were times when the floor was almost perpendicular with the water.

I have seen so many things on this trip that are new to me. We are now in the Bering Sea and there seems to be many whales. Yesterday one was seen almost half out of the water and it was about eighty feet long. One has to see such things to believe them.

I have had quite a good time, too. There are many Alaska people on board and they are very friendly. Then too, there are about seventy soldiers on board and several have taken it upon themselves to see that I am well entertained. We have a victrola on the boat which goes from morning 'til night.

You know, it's not nearly as cold up here as I thought it would be. I imagined there would be snow in Nome now but they say it doesn't start until November.

Will write more later.

Love, Marion

Golden Gate Hotel
Nome, Alaska
October 4, 1920

Dear Folks,

Here I am some 3,000 miles from Seattle. We arrived at Nome soon after midnight last night but did not come ashore until this morning. I will leave for Council early tomorrow morning with the mail. It is a two-day trip and tomorrow night should find me at Solomon.

You should have seen them land us. There are no docks here because of the ice and the steamer can come only about three miles from shore. Some men came out in a gasoline launch to the side of the steamer, then a big rope was put around our shoulders and we climbed down a rope ladder as near as we could to the launch. When the waves washed the launch near enough to the steamer the men grabbed us and threw us into the launch, just like chunks of pork! The water was getting rough and threw salt water all over us so we were soaking wet as well. Now I am sitting by the radiator trying to dry out. There is one thing about salt water; they tell me you get soaked and still not take cold.

This surely is a barren looking country. Not a tree in sight; nothing but snow-topped mountains. It's a funny little town too. Not really so little, but queer houses all packed in together, and board streets.

The steamer does not return for two weeks so you will probably get two letters from me at the same time as I will write again from Council.

There were a number of teachers on the boat and we had much sympathy for each other.

Love, from Marion

Chapter II

Parkas and Mukluks

Marion was fast to become initiated in the ways of the far North. A fashionable young lady, the Alaskan fashions of parkas, mukluks and fur trousers came as a "broadening" blow.

She begins to adjust to a new home and a limited social life - a once-a-week movie. But a sense of humor and a first dog sled ride can count for much, especially when the population of an entire town is making an effort to keep the new teacher happy.

Council, Alaska
October 10, 1920

Dear Folks,

Well, this long, long journey is ended and tomorrow I begin my work. I have a nice little schoolhouse, the best of books, paper, pens, pencils - everything a teacher could wish for. This is really just a country school you know, even though it is in a small town. I have all grades, kindergarten through eighth, but as I just have to teach, it isn't so bad. There is a janitor to do all the manual labor. The school house doesn't look like much on the outside but it is furnace-heated and gas-lighted. You realize that there are only about four hours of daylight here in the winter so I have to teach with artificial lights.

I have a nice place to stay in the Kane House, the only hotel this town boasts. The people are very kind and I have the best of meals which are cooked by the owner's wife, Mrs. Bahlke. I am getting fat already. It seems so good not to have to get up at six and fix breakfast or start the washing, etc. before going to school. And even after paying for my trip, my board and my clothes I can save more here than if I had stayed in the States. Eighteen hundred is no little salary. Everything is very dear here, of course. I am going to wear out all my old clothes up here and have a whole new outfit when I come back next summer.

Did I tell you that it wasn't necessary for me to take another exam in order to teach here. I was granted an Alaska certificate by just showing my old certificate. I expect to enjoy my year here very much.

Everybody says I will never leave Alaska but I'm going to fool them. There are so many men here and so few women that the women all get married. Almost every woman in this town was once a school teacher here.

I had quite a rough trip to Council from Nome. We

should have made the trip in two days but the weather and roads were so bad that it took three days. We bumped along in an old lumber wagon that they call a stage. It was pulled by two horses and two mules. I surely was glad to reach Council. I am pretty well rested now.

I never saw so many dogs in my life. They are big and some are beauties. I am looking forward to having some dog sled rides this winter. Mr. Johnson, Deputy Marshall here in Council, has the finest team and has promised me rides already. He took it upon himself to see that I arrived safely in Council. When I landed in Nome he made sure that I was well cared for. He took me to dinner first, and on Monday night he took me to the movies and treated me to ice cream. Then on Tuesday he took me to breakfast, fixed up an outfit of furs for me from his own wardrobe and also borrowed some so that I wouldn't freeze, gave me a box of candy and saw me safely on my journey.

After I had donned parka, mukluks, fur trousers and mittens I could hardly waddle, let alone walk.

Parkas have no seams and come to or just below the knees. They slip over the head and the hood fits tight to your face with a fringe of long wolverine fur to keep out wind and frost. Some of them are really works of art. The natives make most of them out of squirrel skins. The belly of the squirrel is used on the inside and fur is the outside. The canvas covering is just to keep the squirrel fur dry as the fur tends to come out if it gets wet.

Some of the parkas are made from duck skins. The feathers are turned to the inside and they are real warm. The only problem is they make everybody look like a great fat person. There are also reindeer skin parkas but they are quite heavy.

Up here they tan the furs with sourdough. They use sourdough for yeast, drinking and all kinds of things.

Sourdough is simply flour and water that has fermented.

Mukluks are big fur boots that come above the knee and are about five times the size of your feet. I wore three pairs of mittens, two of socks, an aviation cap and my winter coat under a reindeer fur parka and a canvas parka on top to keep the fur one dry. I also wore fur trousers under my dress and mukluks. Believe me, I didn't get cold! I could have made real use of a derrick to get into the wagon - and I looked like a real Eskimo.

Mr. Johnson is coming over to Council in a few weeks, after the snow comes. That means some free dog sled rides for me. Everyone treats me so nicely here. I guess they are afraid I'll do the same as the last teacher that came. She took one look at Council, turned right around and caught the stage back to Nome.

There really isn't much here. The town proper probably has about thirty people and there must be about fifty miners back in the hills.

When we first got here we had to ford the river and the water came way up to the wagon bottom. There was a man on the Council side with a lantern guiding us across. It was just as exciting as it sounds.

The scows from below Council are pulled up the river by a horse. Once they arrive here the horse is loaded aboard and it all floats downstream in fine fashion.

I got quite a write-up in the daily bulletin beginning like this - "Miss Marion Campbell, a modest-appearing little lady with big blue eyes and a friendly smile, arrived on the stage Thursday having come all the way from Chicago to teach our school this term" --and some more about my not having had time to go home to bid my folks goodbye, my teaching in Chicago and my visiting the school room on Friday.

Alaska is a land of rivers, creeks and great gold mines. I saw all kinds of gold mining between Nome and Council, also some whales and seals. There are no fur seals in this part of the country. They are the hair seals up here. This is also where ermine furs come from and I, of course, am going to try and get some before I come back.

There is every indication that at one time this was a tropical country. When I come home I will tell you all about it.

The water in the Bering Sea is so low now the *Victoria* is unable to unload yet.

Much love, Marion

Council, Alaska
October 13, 1920

Dear Folks,

Just a few lines since I have a chance to send more letters before the *Victoria* sails.

I have been teaching for three days now and like it very much. I have only nine scholars so far, all half-breeds, and very nice children. They are so much easier to handle than the class I had in Chicago last year and from all reports they like me too because I smile all the time.

I am the only young person in the town so it would be lonesome if I did not have work to do. Mrs. Bahlke, where I stay, is a very nice lady and treats me just like a daughter. The men up here respect women so much that they are always good to them. I have been here only ten days and have had two boxes of candy given me. I don't even know who gave me the last one. It was on the table in my room when I came home tonight.

It seems queer to think that I have been gone a month and not had a word from home yet. But the time is going fast and I hope to hear soon.

Alaska is nothing like I expected it to be. I thought

it would be an uncivilized place with no educated people, but it is somewhat different. Two of the women were once school teachers here.

Would you ever believe that the water in a sea like the Bering Sea could go down? It has and that's partly why the *Victoria* has stayed so long. First it was so stormy that she couldn't unload, then the water went down making it impossible for the small boats to get out to her.

I must tell you about the Northern Lights. They are directly overhead and make a funny crackling sound. I can't tell you how beautiful they are. We have wonderful moonlight nights here, almost as light as day, light enough for me to read in my room with very little trouble.

There is very little snow here as yet but the rivers are freezing over and it is quite cold. I do not mind it yet.

I saw my first live reindeer today, a herd that they were butchering. But they were so far away I couldn't see them very plainly. I have seen some quite closely - on a platter though - and it's very good eating. It sells as venison in the states and for something like seventy-five cents a pound.

Mrs. Bahlke is a wonderful cook and I have the best of everything to eat. Of course we do not have fresh milk here but I am becoming accustomed to the canned variety now.

I think one of the strangest things I've realized since coming here is that the children do not know what cows are. But then I suppose they could not be expected to know any more about cows than I did about reindeer.

As soon as my trunks come I will take some pictures to send you so you can tell what kind of a school I have and what the children look like in their parkas. They make a picture all right and they are the cutest looking things when only about two years old with a parka that comes to the ground.

This is a good place to save money once one gets here. I have spent only seventy-five cents since I arrived. Of course there will be my board at the end of the month but that only amounts to seventy-five dollars. There is only one store here and that has nothing I need.

I forgot to tell you what happened on the way over here from Nome the other day. The roadway was just a sort of path along the seacoast and after we had gone about twelve miles we stopped at the little burg of Safety where we stayed overnight. The lodge was run by a Swede who has an Eskimo wife and she showed me to my room and then pointed to the outside privy. All it amounted to was a frame and a door. The wind had blown the sides off, or perhaps someone had kicked the boards off for kindling wood. At any rate, it was quite an experience for a greenhorn like me.

There were some Lapp reindeer herders and some Eskimos in Safety when I was there. The Eskimos looked so fierce in their fur parkas and wolf trimmings that I piled all the furniture in my room against the door that night. When the folks here at Council were told about it they had quite a laugh because the Eskimos wouldn't hurt a flea.

Will close for now. With love from

                                        Marion

Council, Alaska
November 11, 1920

Dear Folks,

How is everybody? l am fine and not frozen up yet. In fact it is raining today and has been for several days. Some people at the hotel tried to get me to carry an umbrella this morning. All they wanted was a good chance to laugh but I am fast learning the ways of the country. It may well be snowing by noon.

I had my first dog sled ride last Saturday. The only complaint I have is that it wasn't long enough. Little Aron, one of my scholars, was with me and every time we hit a bump he almost turned a backwards somersault. I sat in the back all bundled up in furs so I was all right. The driver stood on the runners behind. They talk to the dogs just like horses except that instead of "get up" they say "mush."

The days are shortening up fast now. Daylight does not come in the morning until half past seven and it begins to turn dark by half past two. I teach from two-thirty 'til four by lamplight now. The thermometer has been down to fourteen below zero but it is not very cold now. My barometer is registering a storm and so I suppose it will come. It just might be inside the school house though. The barometer at the hotel registered a storm the other day and we made fun of it, telling Mr. Bahlke the glass was no good. But Mrs. Bahlke said it was all right - there had been a terrible storm in the kitchen all morning!

We did have an awful windstorm here the other night and no one went to bed. Everyone was afraid the house would blow down. It did blow the front off an old store. The wind surely is fierce here.

Five weeks of school gone now and I have been gone from Chicago for eight weeks. The time just flies up here.

I go to the movies every Saturday night. They are shown in the Arctic Brotherhood Hall. They have a hole under the floor where a gasoline engine is used to generate electricity for the projector and lights. Most of the films are old and break a lot but no one minds.

If it's nice weather I stay out all day Saturday and Sunday. Last Sunday I went out at noon and never came home until supper time.

I have had no mail as yet but if the weather stays nice the first overland mail should arrive the twenty-third of this month. I know you have all heard from me by this time for the *Victoria* arrived in Seattle the first of November. You may be sure I am anxious to hear from you.

Everyone is trying to persuade me that I should stay two years. It really would be the sensible thing to do. If I stay another year I can save a thousand dollars, while if I only stay one year I will make about three hundred after paying all expenses, including my return home. But then, maybe I won't want to stay.

This letter will reach you about Christmas time. I am not able to send you any Christmas presents at present (ha!), but will do so later if I can. I am not very flush with money right now but I can wish you a very Merry Christmas and a Happy New Year. Perhaps next year I will be with you. If not, then the year after at the most.

Much love to all,

Marion

Chapter III

Alaskan Sourdough

Marion's first Christmas in Alaska must have been somewhat lonely - but four months of being the only single girl in town must also have brought some compensations.

As the story goes on we see Marion become a full-fledged Alaskan Sourdough. In order to qualify for this honor, one must see the ice flow in during the fall and out the following spring. She was duly initiated.

We also learn of Council's biggest event of the year - the Kamoogan Races. A timed dog sled race between Nome and Council (a distance of 85 miles), it was necessary for the winning team to arrive at the finish line with every dog that started - be they dead or alive.

And, too, our young friend makes her decision to stay "just one more year."

Council, Alaska
December 11, 1920

Dear Mother and all,

Received your letter written October third on December the third, so you see it takes some time for mail to reach me. Also received some written the ninth of October. Tom is a faithful correspondent and so I get two letters from him in each mail.

Yes, we do get some fresh fruit up here: apples, oranges and grapefruit. I am not living on fish but eat quite a bit of reindeer and ptarmigan. My board is sixty-five dollars a month and ten for a room so I ought to do pretty well when it comes to eats. I have been having a bad cold. There is rather an epidemic here.

Nine weeks of school finished and I've been gone from Chicago over three months. Time is flying and I'll soon be back home, unless I decide to stay for two years. I do not mind the cold up here. We bundle up and just take it. I have a pair of reindeer mukluks that were given to me and a pair of mittens. The mittens are real beauties - wolf skin, all lined with squirrel and beaded. They are gauntlets and come to my elbow.

In two weeks it will be Christmas, then we'll see what Marion has. There are a lot of bachelors up here and I could work them for anything, I believe. All I have to do is say I'm going to get this or that and they race to see who can be the first to get it for me. They treat me like a little kid.

There have been a couple of blizzards but no bad ones yet. There is not enough snow. When a lot of loose snow falls and a wind comes up - oh, my - one can't see ten feet ahead.

Love, from Marion

Council, Alaska
December 31, 1920

Dear Folks,

The last day of the year and it is also the last day of my third month of school. I am wondering all the time what you folks are doing and how you are. The letters are so old when I get them that it's hard to tell.

I took no Christmas vacation and am trying to shorten time that way. Yet the last weekend was horribly long. I dismissed school at noon Friday and spent a good share of the afternoon filling Christmas stockings. In the evening I had to run the program and after that I just enjoyed myself.

I received fifteen Christmas presents, I think. Anyway, I got a mirror, handkerchiefs, fancy bag, tam-o-shanter, Eskimo picture, two little gold nuggets, a toilet set, two bottles of perfume, a fancy dress hanger, sachet folder, towel, four boxes of candy and a doll. Wasn't that enough? Then today I won a box of candy on how to spell ptarmigan.

The mail should be in tomorrow but as it's a holiday I suppose it won't come until Sunday or Monday. When it gets so close I can hardly wait. I always get so much.

Last night the thermometer dropped to thirty degrees below zero. It's frosty today but not windy so I don't mind it so much.

There doesn't seem to be much to tell any more. I'm working every day; the weekends are long and I sleep most of the time then. I'm fatter than I've been in a long time and look and feel fine. The country or the job agrees with me.

Love to everybody,

Marion

Council, Alaska
January 12, 1921

Dear Leonard,

Read in the bulletin that the first over-land mail did not arrive in Seattle until January 6. That means you are just beginning to get my over-land letters and it will be the fifteenth of March before you get this one. I get mail quite regularly now. Saturday will be time for it again and I am looking forward to it.

We have been having a blizzard for the past four days and some times the snow flies so thick it's impossible to see six feet ahead.

We had quite a fire scare here last night. Just as we were going to bed at eleven o'clock, Mrs. Bahlke and I saw a fire from her window. The wind was blowing the sparks and flames in every direction. We called to the men who were playing cards downstairs and they all ran with buckets and shovels. Here everyone is a fireman. When they came back they said it was only a pile of ashes burning behind the school house but there was a possible danger of setting the school, a boat and another house on fire.

Last week there was a house fire and as usual every one turned out with their buckets. They formed a bucket brigade down to the river and had the fire out in a short time.

How is everybody? I hope you are all well. I often wonder what kind of a winter you are having in Michigan.

Love, Marion

Council, Alaska
February 10, 1921

Dear Folks,

The box which you sent has not arrived yet but will probably come in the next mail. Jessie sent me a pair of stockings in the last mail.

It has been storming for the past four days and when it lasts over three days it generally means we're in for two weeks of the same. Actually, there is very little snow as yet.

Today is Mrs. Bahlke's birthday so there is to be a party tonight (we take advantage of any excuse for one).

Last Sunday Mr. Bahlke took me out for a dog sled ride. We only went about three miles down the river and came to an overflow so had to turn around. Since it was three below zero that was far enough for me. I wore Mrs. Bahlke's parka and as she weighs two hundred and twenty-five pounds, you can imagine the fit!

I am making my first deposit in the bank now. All my bills are paid and I have a hundred and thirty round iron bones for the first deposit. A bank in Tacoma failed the other day and caused quite a scare here but we've gotten over it. I'm sending my money to Nome. I am getting to be a real miser and don't spend a cent unless I have to. A bath in the bathtub costs a dollar here so I don't get one more than twice a month, if I get one that often. It raises my board bill.

Yesterday was beastly cold, about 40 degrees below zero. I am beginning the second half of my school year this week and I haven't missed a day of school so far this year. Will have a vacation in a few days - Washington's birthday. By the time you get this letter we will be having no darkness. You will have no snow but we will be wading in it up to our necks.

I have been promised a dog sled ride for every day in April but that's not saying I will get it. Am looking forward to spring. They say it is a wonderful time here in Alaska. Everything grows so quickly once it starts because of sunshine and daylight all the time.

I hear that there are a hundred pounds of mail coming up today so am very much in hopes my Christmas presents will come.

Am well. Hardly a cold this winter, so you see this is a healthy climate.

Many happy returns of March 12 and 24 for my dear sister and Mama. I know this will reach you late but forgot to mention it before now. I think I am to be initiated as an Alaska Sourdough on my birthday.

Love, from Marion

Council, Alaska
May 15, 1921

Dear Father, Mother and all,

It's a long, long time since I have written and an awful long time since I've had a letter - am living in hopes of getting one soon. The *S.S. Victoria* does not leave Seattle until the seventh of June this year so it will be almost the first of July before the mail on her gets here. The *Bear* should be here the eighth though, so since she carries mail too we hope to get some here in Council.

I am a true Alaskan Sourdough now as we have had several ice runs. There was one today. The ice has gone out slowly so there has been no flood yet. The Niukluk River is some river, rather swift, and my room is almost over it. At night I lay awake and listen to the roar. It is a real sight to see the ice go out, big chunks climbing and bumping against each other.

There is one house down by the river that has big hooks coming out of the ceiling. Every time the river gets too high they hang all the furniture on the hooks. They even hang their piano and davenport up there. One time a huge chunk of ice came right through their wall and filled the whole kitchen. I would prefer a friendly ice man myself!

The snow is not nearly gone yet but the wild flowers are blooming on the hilltops. There are the most wonderful pussy willows here; some are two inches long.

We have no darkness now, though it does get a little like dusk. Every blind has to be drawn and pinned to the casement in order to get a little sleep.

Only two more weeks of school after this one. Next year I will be finished on the nineteenth of May instead of the first of June so I will make the first boat out. I am going to Nome for several weeks this summer to have my teeth fixed. I go about the first of June. Now I see where I spend some money.

There has been no frost for two days and today the wind is in the south so the dredges will soon be starting. I am going out to see how they work.

We have had quite some excitement in Council since I wrote last. The twentieth of April we had a Kamoogan race from Nome to Council. Kamoogan is the Eskimo word for dog. There were eight teams that came over, the largest turnout they have ever had here for a race. Council gave the winners a large silver cup which surprisingly was won by a team driven by women. The teams arrived here in Council between ten a.m. and twelve noon on Friday. They did nothing the rest of the day but on Saturday there was a race for ladies only. They wanted me to drive a team but I was afraid I couldn't manage even the five dogs which the ladies were allowed, so they made me official starter. I was glad I didn't enter the race for most of the women came in bruised and scratched and some even lost their teams.

This is a great country for game and this spring I had my first wild goose. It tasted very good. They also have ducks and cranes which they use for food.

The ice is all gone from the river now. The revenue cutter *Bear* arrived in Nome yesterday and the *Victoria* leaves Seattle today - so you see Alaska is beginning to wake up for the summer.

School will be over next week. Oh joy! This has been some long term. Glad for a rest.

Love to all, Marion

Nome, Alaska
July 19, 1921

Dear Helen,

Your letter of June 23 just received and I was surely glad to hear from you.

I spend very little on meals since my admirers are so willing to provide them for me. I'm having the time of my life here. It's worth something to be the only single girl in a town. You're right, I just may be coming home on my honeymoon. I had my fortune told the other day and the woman said she saw me facing marriage. Tom finally has given up on me so I'm free now.

More love, Marion

Council, Alaska
August 30, 1921

Dear Jessie,

Well, you see I am back at my old stamping ground again. Only six more days of grace and I begin the old grind. I'm going down the river on a three-day trip tomorrow though, if the weather is nice.

Today is a big day. The scows are up the river, the

mail is in and it is outside mail. I received a pile of letters so next out-going mail day will see me busy.

I went on a trip to Teller this summer. Teller is about a hundred and forty miles up the coast from Nome, a twelve-hour run in the boat we used. I went with a girl from Nome to visit her sister who teaches there. I've met most of the girls who teach in Seward Peninsula now.

Mr. and Mrs. Bahlke have sold out and so our new landlord is Jake Nelson. We're going to miss Mrs. Bahlke's excellent cooking.

Council seems so dead after Nome and Nome isn't much.

The food up here is getting me and I'm getting thinner and thinner. Soon I'll have to stand twice in the same place to cast a shadow. I like good meat and that's something we don't have here in Alaska in the summer. It all has a cold-storage taste. I did pretty well in Nome on chicken and steaks but they didn't last long enough. We are getting curlew, duck and ptarmigan now and they taste good.

You should see the gardens here. Turnips, beets, radishes and lettuce that couldn't be bettered anywhere.

The days are shortening up fast now, dark at eight and not light until four. Cloudy weather makes them seem even shorter.

I am planning to start school the sixth of September this year and be out early so I can come out on the first boat in the spring.

Am sending you a few pictures taken here in Council. I don't remember having sent you any before.

The blueberries, cranberries and currants are ripe now. The blueberries are the same as huckleberries but not quite as sweet; the cranberries are smaller than the outside cranberries, about the size of the huckleberry.

Love to all, Marion

Chapter IV

Enter Romance

We are now introduced to Fred, Marion's favored suitor. Her boast of leaving Alaska after one year is no longer a topic of her conversation and we see her accept the possibility of becoming "just another Alaskan housewife."

The glamor of her Alaska adventure changes to reality as she sees the temperature drop to 40 degrees below zero and the telephone lines go down for 25 days.

But Marion moves on into her second school year undaunted. She introduces heretofore unheard of parties and celebrations to this quiet little town and creates a Christmas program with only five pupils.

All this and wedding plans too!

Council, Alaska
September 19, 1921

Dear Folks,

Just one more summer mail after this one and then
no more mail until after Christmas. So I suppose I must
write good, long letters.

We are having the most glorious weather now.
There is very little rain and the sunshine is wonderful.
Everything is red and brown and the birds are turning
white. We are having very heavy frosts now and the
natives expect an early winter.

I spent the last two days out on the creek at the
Northern Light Mining Camp. We tramped around the
different mines and I came back to town with a regular
appetite. Next Saturday I am going on a fourteen mile
hike up Melsing Creek to see a mine where they sluice.
I have seen a sluice dredge and a hydraulic mine work
and watched the men pan out gold, all very interesting.

We are beginning our third week of school. Time
certainly goes faster when one is working.

I sent out on the last boat for quite a little
embroidery work and I'm going to send for more on the
next one. I have to have something constructive to do.

Everyone has been asking me why I stayed another
year so I may as well 'fess up. I have been engaged for
some time. I didn't come home because Fred couldn't get
away for another year so I thought I would stay and
teach this year to be near him. We will either be married
this Christmas vacation or not for another year. If we
wait until later, I want to come home to be married. We
will most likely be married this year though, for the hotel
is apt to close any time and then I won't have a home.
Fred is terribly worried that you folks won't like him; he
is quite a bit older than I am and he'd rather not marry
until he finds out if my family will approve of him. He's
rather in a pickle, wouldn't you say?

If I marry Fred I won't have to worry about grocery money or whether or not I can afford a new dress. We would like to be married on December 28 but of course it's not settled yet.

Fred is not really handsome but he has the beautiful brown eyes Helen used to rave about. His hair is thinning on top but looks don't make the man, do they? I'm sure you'll all be nice to the husband I bring home. But we aren't even married yet and here I am, counting my chickens before they're hatched. Now isn't this a nice surprise to spring on you?

Well, how is the farm doing now? I am anxious to see it and everybody on it.

The mail is coming in now and it is almost nine o'clock. I won't get mine until noon though unless Mr. Kinne takes pity on me and sends it over sooner.

Well, I must close as I have about fourteen more letters to write.

Love, from Marion

Council, Alaska
September 21, 1921

Dear Helen,

Your long letter just came and it surely was nice to get. You do write the most interesting letters.

I was going to keep my engagement for a surprise until I came out but I decided that since I might be married this winter, I'd better tell. We will probably be married during the Christmas holiday but the date seems to change with the weather. I have been engaged since the sixth of May, quite close to your wedding day, so I have kept the secret pretty well, you see. I have only told one person here in Council but I suppose they all know it now since that person likes to be the bearer of news.

I am going to send out on this mail for a new white lace or crepe dress and all the fixings so if I do get married here it won't have to be in one of my new embroidered nighties, nice as they are.

You may be sure I'm very busy embroidering, crocheting and sewing but my hope chest isn't very full yet. I have a few towels, spoons, three nightgowns, enough linen for several tablecloths and sets of napkins and a few things like that. Oh yes, I have two new corsets, not worn yet.

When I get married I'm going to have obey left out of the ceremony because I won't and he'll have to anyhow. Guess we'll have a honeymoon trip of some kind a year or so afterwards. We plan on spending two weeks with every friend and relative we have and that will take about a year; then we can begin again. The only trouble with such business is that it takes too much railroad fare.

You must be thin all right if you only weigh 118 pounds for I weigh almost that myself.

Gee, it seems ages since I've seen all of you. We'll have a great reunion when I come home, won't we?

I expect my new fur in on the next boat. Won't I be dolled up though in it and my blue georgette!

Well, I must quit this scrawling and get to work.

Love, Marion

Council, Alaska
October 12, 1921

Dear Father, Mother and all,

It looks like there might be another mail to go outside after all. The *Victoria* had a bad trip last time and hasn't left for the outside yet. Of course I can't be sure this mail will reach her before she leaves.

The rivers are freezing over fast this year, much earlier than last. Most of the dredges have shut down and none can run more than a week longer.

I am trying to interest the people in having a box social and plate dinner some night soon to raise money for the Christmas party - and for the fun of it, too. Two of the women here are regular wet blankets though. One has far too much to do; she has a two-room house, two canary birds and a husband to take care of. The other is so fat she can't stand any exertion and she thinks she's sick. If she'd work up a little pep she'd be all right.

Mrs. Taylor, my neighbor, is all energy and we get along fine. I go over to her house and make cakes, wash dishes and dress the babies and the like and she keeps me for Sunday night dinner.

The movies started last Saturday, so there's at least one thing to look forward to each week.

The year is certainly sliding around fast. This is the sixth week of school. So far, most of the time, I have had only five youngsters, the rest of them are out fishing.

I am still spending my time sewing, crocheting and embroidering. I don't want to have to make a mad scramble over Christmas presents this year. Mine will be all ready weeks before, I assure you.

Well, I must quit scribbling. Hope you are all well - I am.

Lots of love, Marion

Council, Alaska
October 26, 1921

Dear Leonard,
This is the last letter you will get by boat from me this year. The rest will go by dog team.

I am planning to have a Halloween party on Monday.

Wish you could be here. We are going to bob for apples in a tub of water; catch apples, hung on a string, with our mouths; hunt nuts; have a peanut race and all the usual Halloween fun-games.

The native kids are riding up and down the street today with their dogs hitched to hand sleds. They have great fun with only one or two dogs. Last winter, nine children were playing with their dogs and went over the bluff - dogs, sled, kids and all. None were seriously hurt but they were all badly scared.

Our doctor is leaving for Nome tonight or tomorrow. I keep teasing him about making the trip to try to get civilized. He's always accusing me of being only half civilized.

Write and tell me all about your school.

Love, from your sister

Marion

Council, Alaska
November 21, 1921

Dear Mother,

Your letter of October 19 came today. I had twelve nice long letters and yours was one of the shortest.

I hear you are doing nicely on the new farm. A year from now, I will be with you for three or four months. How I'm looking forward to it! You can tell Leonard for me that those Chicago farmers he doesn't think much of can still show him a thing or two.

You asked about the dirt in this country. Well, these old log buildings are fierce. I dig out about a bushel every Saturday from my room. Of course the stove in my room makes a lot of the mess.

My boarding place is not very nice this year and I'm glad I have only six or seven months more to put in.

This ends my third month of school and a third of the school year. Next week I begin to work on my Christmas program. That will wear my brains some.

I am invited out for Thanksgiving dinner - turkey and everything. I must help get it too. Mrs. Taylor is my best friend here in town, outside of Fred.

How is everybody? I hope you are all well. I had a cold last week but I'm all right now.

I want to wish you a Merry Christmas and a Happy New Year. I hope Santa brings you lots of nice presents.

Have Helen share her letter with you as I wrote her a little more news.

Lots of love to all,

Marion

Council, Alaska
January 2, 1922

Dear Mother and Father,

Well, another year has begun and it doesn't seem any time at all since it was New Year's a year ago.

I suppose you think I am dead or married or something but I'm not. I was sick for about three weeks before Christmas and missed one out-going mail.

Was Santa Claus good to you? He was to me. I got six boxes of candy, three boudoir caps (which I never wear) a satin camisole, two towels, two handkerchiefs, a ball of crochet cotton and a silver tomato server, a pin and a picture of an Eskimo woman and baby, framed.

Christmas Eve we had an entertainment at A. B. Hall. First we had a program by the school, then movies, Santa Claus and presents, followed with ice cream, cake and coffee. It takes a lot of food to fill up the Eskimos. One woman ate five dishes of ice cream, seven pieces of cake and drank three cups of coffee.

Christmas night Jake (the owner) served a Christmas dinner at the Kane house. We had seven courses; first, oyster soup; second, fish and sauce; third, asparagus salad; fourth, pork and apple sauce; fifth, Turkey, potatoes, cranberries, macaroni and cheese, green beans and peas, parker house rolls and coffee; sixth, ice cream and cake; seventh, oranges, nuts, apples, raisins and more coffee. After dinner we went to the movies and after that Mrs. Taylor served more coffee and we talked until nearly morning.

I had a week's vacation for Christmas and spent most of the time sewing for my hope chest. I wished I had another week. I made a pair of pillow slips and embroidered them, made and embroidered a nightgown and made a pair of bloomers and an apron.

Last night Mrs. Taylor gave a dinner party. There were about a dozen grownups and Mrs. Taylor and I were the only women. We had a fine time, too. We had fruit cocktail, Scotch broth, turkey, mashed potatoes, corn on the cob, escalloped tomatoes, jelly, ice cream, cookies and fruitcake.

How did the new farm do this year? Well, I hope.

We have had a mild winter so far; lots of snow but not very cold. We had a bad blow the day before Christmas. It took down the telephone and electric lines. The cable was down for about a week and then the line between Nome and Council went down or I would have sent you a Christmas telegram. But the broken lines weren't the worst; if it hadn't been for the ice in the Bering Sea, Nome would have been wiped off the map. The water was up into the main street and the ice was pushed right up to the buildings.

The days are so short now that we have lights all day in school. We haven't had any sunshine for weeks.

As I'm sure you've realized by now, I'm not married and probably won't be for almost a year. We are not sure, however. We may be married in June. We would both like to see Seattle and San Francisco together and decide if we want to live in one of those places or back in Minnesota. But nothing is settled yet and we change our minds with the wind. Nevertheless, I will be home sometime in the summer or early fall.

My new fox fur came about a month ago and it sure is a beauty! It is much bigger than my old fur and has a beautiful lining of gold-colored, brocaded satin.

I am beginning my fifth month of school and the year continues to go fast. The people here say time flies until Christmas but slows after that as there is nothing to look forward to. I told them they could look forward to my going away but that didn't seem to suit them. Tommy Taylor says he is going with me. He is some boy. The other day his mother and I were walking down the street with him and he got tired. He pointed to himself and said, "Mother, this thing tired. Pick it up."

Well, I must close but as Helen says, "I will write again before I croak."

Lots of love, Marion

Council, Alaska
January 16, 1922

Dear Mother,
Received your letter of November 13 two weeks ago. You certainly have had an early winter. So far it has been mild here except for about two weeks when the thermometer went down to 40 degrees below zero. Today it is raining.

The telephone line is up at last so we have news now. The wire was down for twenty-five days.

The Kane House boarders had quite a scare about a week ago. Jake told us we had to get out and find a new place by the fifteenth. There was no place to go and after we had worried our brains for a couple of days he decided we could stay after all. It wouldn't bother me much to leave if I could find a place to go. This place is really bad this year and getting worse. I have graduated from eating in the dining room for breakfast and now eat at the counter where all the Eskimos eat. It hurts my feelings and also my bottom. I have to sit on a stool instead of a chair. It is dark in the morning now and Jake refuses to light the gas lanterns so we eat by a coal-oil lamp turned low so it won't smoke. We get salt shakers, broom straws and so on mixed up in our food because he cooks by the light that shines in from the lobby instead of having a light in the kitchen. I wish to goodness there hadn't been such a good crop of cranberries and turnips in Alaska this year as that's about the only fruit and vegetable he gives us.

It's raining one minute today and snowing the next. This is certainly warm weather for this time of year here.

Last night I parted with thirty-two dollars income tax. Then there was another dollar notary fee.

Don't worry about Fred and me coming back to this part of Alaska to live. It is just about dead. I don't know where we are going to live. Most likely near St. Paul or perhaps in Seattle. We won't really know until we get back to the States.

Last Sunday morning I made myself another gingham apron. Fine occupation for Sunday but one has to do something. I was out visiting all afternoon.

I am embroidering a lot of things for my hope chest now. The things are so pretty. I am getting anxious to use them.

The days are lengthening out quite a little now but it is still so dull that we have to have lights all day.

Nothing much to tell. Nothing going on at all.

Love, Marion

Council, Alaska
January 29, 1922

Dear Mother and Father,

Well, I'm not at the Kane House any more. I live in a little three room cabin all alone. I've only been here about a week and I wish I had been here all winter. I have a fine time. Someone is coming in all the time. I am on the main street of the town and every one that goes by stops in. I had more callers in two days than I had at the Kane House all year. Saturday I had three people to lunch, Fred for dinner, and Sunday six people for lunch.

My cabin is made of rough logs, not canvassed or painted or anything inside. None of the houses here are plastered as the frost warps them so. The walls are generally sealed and covered with canvas and calcimined to make them as fireproof as possible. Mine is just the rough logs, rustic style. It is very warm though and comfortably fixed. Everyone was nice and loaned me the things I lacked. I have a kerosene stove and a wood stove both in the kitchen and a dandy heater in the front room. I am invited out almost every evening for dinner.

I am beginning my sixth month of school today and anxious for the next four months to go. There will be about eight other Council people going out on the boat when I go so expect to have a good time.

The days are much longer now. It is daylight by eight in the morning and not dark until almost four in the afternoon.

The reason I left the Kane House is because Jake wouldn't give me my breakfast until half past eight and I was supposed to be in school before then.

It surely would be nice to go to Florida for the winter!

Love, Marion

Council, Alaska
April 2, 1922

Dear Helen,

Your nice letter of January 30 arrived yesterday. I was very glad to hear from you.

Yesterday Fred and I were out to the Northern Light Mine for dinner. Nearly all Council was there. Another man walked out with us. They walked home too but Pearsons gave me a ride back. I stood on the runners and drove the dogs for the first time. It was my first dog sled ride this winter and the first time I have been out of town since snow fell (of which we have about eight feet), but the weather is warm.

There was an Eskimo dog race this morning and of course I bet on the wrong team and lost a box of candy. There is going to be another Kamoogan race this year from Nome to Council just after Easter.

There are only seven weeks more of school now and I'm looking forward to the time of leaving.

Am going to dinner at the dear doctor's tonight. I am out to meals half the time and have someone here the other half. I've gotten so fat since I left the Kane House. Have gained seven or eight pounds in the last ten weeks. Hope I don't keep it up or I'll have to start reducing and how I would hate to have to quit eating!

Hoping this finds you well.

                                        Love from Marion.

Seattle, Washington
August 6, 1922

Dear Mother and Father,

Tomorrow I start east by way of Athens and Salt Lake so I will be home in a few weeks. I suppose you had made up your minds that I was never coming - but a bad penny always returns you know.

Now I must explain about Fred. You are probably wondering why he did not come out with me on this trip as we had planned. The truth is that Fred is a very proud man and when his business went bad this past winter he found he would be unable to provide me with a new house as he had promised. He is determined not to marry until he can provide properly for his wife and so he's gone back to the gold mines to try and get another start. I haven't seen or heard from him for some months now and don't even know where he is so I can write. I never knew Alaska could be so lonely until Fred went away.

All this is hard for me to write about but I will soon be home and we can talk it all out when I get there. Sometimes even ladies of my age long for a mother's shoulder to cry on.

Love to all, Marion

Chapter V

St. Michael - Port of the Yukon

Marion remained home for one year, visiting family and friends and attending some classes. But when school preparations began during the summer of 1923, she decided once again to accept a position in Alaska.

Upon her arrival at Nome, she was assigned to a school in St. Michael, a port city 125 miles to the southeast.

Butler Hotel
Seattle, Washington
August 20, 1923

Dear Helen,

Just a note to let you know how I'm getting along. I have to pack my trunk tonight and tomorrow it goes to the boat. I will be glad to be on my way again. It's been tiresome waiting.

Had a very nice trip here except that it was hot and dusty part of the time. Met some very nice people though and there were quite a few young folks on the train. I managed to lure a nice looking young man into buying my breakfast one morning.

Write when you have time.

Lovingly, Marion

Nome, Alaska
September 1, 1923

Dear Mother,

We are in Nome at last and I expect to be here until sometime tomorrow. We then go to Golovin for a couple of days, then on to St. Michael, my new school assignment. I'll only be a week late in starting school and that isn't so bad.

St. Michael is the port of the Yukon River. It is nineteen miles from the mouth of the Yukon but the mouth is too shallow for a port. It was quite a large town at one time. It used to be a Russian fort and boasted that it was the only fort never captured by the Indians. I guess the reason for that is because there have never been any Indians up here to capture anything. There are only Eskimos around St. Michael and they wouldn't take anything away from anybody.

These Eskimos are the most gentle and honest people I have ever seen. I never lock anything away. They may pick something up and look at it but they always put it right back exactly as it was.

I was seasick for a few hours; at least I thought I was. I had missed breakfast and I've just about decided that I was only hungry since at noon I was nearly starved and ate an enormous lunch. I've been stuffing myself ever since. The meals on this boat are very good. We've had turkey, goose and chicken dinners. They tell me there's to be a regular Thanksgiving dinner for us so we should have turkey again tomorrow.

There are only two other passengers for St. Michael, a very old lady and an Eskimo girl. There were several passengers that I knew quite well and some very nice girls on board. There was also a regular mob of teachers, nurses and missionaries.

Bahlkes sent word out for me to come ashore and have dinner tonight. If there wasn't any danger of being left behind, I will go in.

Must leave now, Marion

St. Michael, Alaska
September 8, 1923

Dear Jessie,

I am sure you have heard all about my trip from the folks so all I will say is that it was very nice and I thoroughly enjoyed it.

I didn't go ashore in Nome until the second day I was there and when I did go I was sorry I hadn't gone before. I was greeted by everyone like a long-lost brother (or should I say sister?) I received several invitations to dinner, some boxes of candy, and nearly had my arm shaken off. It was almost like coming home.

I am boarding here in St. Michael with a widow lady, Mrs. Moses, who lives alone most of the time with a cat, a dog and a canary. The dog is a beauty, a thoroughbred Spitz, white as snow. His name is Laddie. He is as intelligent as he is handsome, too. The cat's name is Hootch. Mrs. Moses may go out on the sailing and if she does I'll rent her house and keep the cat.

There hasn't been a frost here as yet so everything is still green. The berries are just getting ripe but the crop is a poor one this year.

School will begin next Monday. They gave me the first week off with pay to get settled. It looks as though I'll have a dandy school board to work for.

Please write as often as you can. The mail service is so slow way up here that if we only respond to each other's previous letter we won't write many. Mail leaves here every week. It takes quite a while to get out but still it goes. It is taken up the Yukon and then out to Seattle over land. I usually get mail every week, too.

Love, Marion

St. Michael, Alaska
October 12, 1923

Dear Margaret,

Almost time for school but I have a few moments and I must make use of them. The last boat will be in in four or five days and then no more mail for several weeks as none leaves here until the first of November.

We have been having some very cold weather but it is not so very bad today. The days are getting short already, they were so long six weeks ago when I came.

This is the end of my sixth week of the school year. It will be six weeks Sunday morning since I arrived here in St. Mike. It looks to be quite a town from the sea.

There is the wireless up on a hill, then an Indian village, next is the bureau school building, then the white village, the post, and then another native village. It is spread out so it looks like quite a large place. The beach is piled with wharves and old boats and there are dozens of river boats, nice big ones, going to ruin. I suppose they will lay there and rot, it would cost so much to fix them up now.

There has been some talk of having a naval training station here next year and if it goes through it will mean that St. Mike will be a real town again.

It is recess now and I'm famished already. I don't eat any breakfast as Mrs. Moses doesn't get up until almost noon. I don't care as I don't like to get up early anyway, just soon enough to get to school on time. I know I won't get up for breakfast even when she's gone. It will be lonesome here when she leaves so I am planning to keep her cat and dog this winter for company.

Just had a fuss with my newest pupil. He doesn't want to do one thing I tell him, so I made him mind me and he set up a howl. This is the way it sounded: "I want my maw maw! Yow! Yow! Yow!" My, how I love the little cross-eyed rascal. If that has sarcastic overtones, I'm glad they came through. That really isn't very nice but I'm getting so I hate a scene in the school room. It spoils the reputation that I have established for temper and discipline. Everyone in town thinks I have an easy temper in the school room but they don't know how I boil inside sometimes!

October 13, Saturday Afternoon

Saturday is my day of luxury. I stayed in bed until noon today and am going for a walk soon. The sun is shining and it is simply wonderful out. The wind is blowing but this is the first sunshine we've had in weeks.

I've been cleaning my room and getting my things straightened out. I wash one Saturday, iron the next and mend the next. I don't do anything in the evening but embroider, crochet, read and thump on the piano. Just at present I'm trying to get my letter writing done before the boat gets in. We expect her in about Wednesday and I've only got six letters written so far.

I will be a widow soon now. I sure hate to see Mrs. Moses go. For one thing, I hate the idea of having to do my own cooking. But dear Mrs. Moses has made me two fruit cakes for Thanksgiving and Christmas.

Lovingly, Marion

St. Michael, Alaska
October 23, 1923

Dear Helen,

Your letters of August 11, September 13 and September 26 all arrived about ten days ago. Through some mistake I didn't get the one sent to me on the steamer so it just came with the others.

The last *Vic* has come and gone. The *Buford* was expected this week but she refuses to come. Another boat was supposed to start from Nome this morning but she is high and dry on the beach so a small boat from here is going. There are seven passengers here for the outside and two for Nome. They all turned down the *Vic* for the *Buford* and now they may be stuck. It's quite stormy now and there is no knowing whether they will be able to get outside or not.

The Japan earthquake didn't affect us here at all. It may have made the sea rough but it is so rough most of the time anyway, we probably wouldn't have noticed it.

So my friend Doris is to be married. It looks like all the old gang is going to beat me. It seems like everyone I ever knew is either married or about to be.

No, Helen, there are no snakes up here but there are

plenty of mice. Didn't I tell you about their playing tag over my bedroom floor at Council? I'd turn my flashlight on them but they were so arrogant they just looked at me and went on with their games.

Well, it's time to call the young angels to order and try to impart a small portion of knowledge to them. I sometimes feel that it's a mighty small portion.

It is trying to snow today but isn't succeeding very well though there is a strong north wind blowing. We've had some quite cold weather but last week was quite nice.

I had twenty letters on the last mail, including two from girls I met while at school. I won't get any more now until about the first of December, then I expect a heap of it.

I have really been spending some exciting evenings. I now have a seventeen-piece luncheon set and a buffet set with crocheted edges. I also have an embroidered card table cover. Aren't you envious?

Dear Helen, I don't know what I want for Christmas; most anything would be acceptable. But don't worry about Christmas presents for me. As far as magazines are concerned my next door neighbor takes the Ladies Home Journal, Pictorial, Saturday Evening Post, Priscilla, Pathfinder and the newspapers. I take a geography magazine and another woman in town Cosmopolitan and the Red Book, and one of the stores keeps magazines, so I am quite well off for reading matter. You might send me something to embroider.

I'm planning to splurge on some new duds when I get my debts paid. It's going to cost me at least sixty a month to live here though, maybe more.

Write whenever you have time. I have to get to work now. I've given the darlings twenty minutes recess, twice too much. I do so want to get these letters ready for the boat though and I still have four or five to write.

Much love, Marion

Chapter VI

Captain Olsen

When Marion returned to Alaska she met Kaurin Olsen, a Master Mariner and captain of a supply boat on the Yukon. Kaurin was a shy, quiet man but in the limited social environment of St. Michael soon became well acquainted with Marion. The result of their friendship is amply explained in the letters that follow.

St. Michael, Alaska
November 1, 1923

Dear Mother,

Just a few lines to let you know that I am fine. I'm a busy woman again as I have a fair sized house to keep clean and my own cooking to do. Coal is so much dirtier than wood that one can hardly keep a place presentable. I don't get up early enough in the morning so I have it all to do at night and Saturday is a busy day. I am doing my own bread baking also. Baked last Saturday for the first time in four or five years. It is edible but not so very wonderful. I also baked a cake and a ham and made a custard last night for my lunch today. Don't I sound domesticated?

The weather hasn't turned cold here yet. Yesterday was like spring and today it is raining.

The boats have all gone south. The little boat that took people from here to Nome to catch the *Buford* had trouble and the *Buford* had to tow her back to St. Mike.

The children had a fine time playing Halloween pranks last night. One boy fell in the bay. He had his arithmetic book in his mouth and never lost it, but he was well soaked from the looks of the book this morning. They rang all the bells and had a good time blocking doorways.

The weekly winter mail from here has started already. I will get mail six days quicker here than at Council and of course it will be that much faster getting out.

I suppose you have heard that St. Mike is the sailor town for the Yukon boats. Well, it certainly is and I am now being courted by a Captain Kaurin Olsen of the Northern Commercial Company. He is very nice but don't worry, we have no plans along the line of matrimony.

Well, I will close. It is half past two now and nearly

dark already. I hope you all have a Merry Christmas and a Happy New Year.

Lovingly, Marion

St. Michael, Alaska
December 10, 1923

Dear Helen,
The time is going fast and I'm not getting any letters. There have been three winter mails so far and no letters for me so I am writing to all my relatives and telling what I think of them. Guess I'll have to marry an Eskimo to get some attention. Then I'd have to start fishing for tomcod and go seal hunting (reflecting on my last sentence, I've decided just to wait until the folks at home feel like writing!)

The children are playing "Ruth and Jacob" and I got into the ring and fooled the youngster that was blindfolded. You should have seen his face when he discovered who it was.

It sure is cold here now; has been down below zero for the past ten days. My house is as cold as an iceberg and water freezes on the stove even with a fire burning. I woke myself up shivering this morning.

I'm trying to get some Christmas presents made for my school children but am not making much progress. Have only made four aprons so far. Guess I'll make some camisoles for some of the girls. They'll be quicker.

Just thought of a name for your dog if you haven't named her yet. You might call her Alaska. That's a girl's name.

Love to all, Marion

St. Michael, Alaska
January 7, 1924

Dear Mother,

I know you are all anxious to know the how, why and wherefore of this sudden wedding. I hardly know myself; it all happened so quickly.

We announced our engagement the 27th of December and everyone said, "Why don't you get married during your vacation and save money." So we did. Mrs. Evans was giving a New Year's party and it was turned into a wedding. Only those in the wedding knew about it. Mr. Evans was best man and Mrs. Hickman was my maid of honor. Mr. Williams, the commissioner, read the ceremony.

We had to wear nearly all old clothes, no chance to get new things. I did have a few new ones. I wore my white dress and white slippers and stockings. Kaurin had a very good looking brown suit that he hadn't worn very much. He says he had new socks and handkerchief.

Some of the people didn't know there was going to be a wedding until I came down the stairs. I had hoped to pull it off as a big surprise and it was certainly successful.

Mrs. Evans served a dandy supper and the table was very pretty. Mrs. Williams made the wedding cake a piece of which you will get in time. It won't be good to eat by then but I wanted you to have a souvenir of my wedding. It is a real travelling cake as one piece also goes to Norway to Kaurin's people.

We had a wire of congratulations from Kaurin's mother and brothers in Norway Saturday and one from Jessie yesterday. I guess we surprised quite a few people.

The people here have had quite a time getting the right name for me. Most of them make a slip and call me Miss Campbell once in a while.

I had two weeks vacation but really don't feel much

as though I had any. My Christmas program broke into it first and then of course Christmas itself. Then Kaurin gave a party on Thursday evening after Christmas to announce our engagement. His party was at my house so I had all the work to do. Then the next four days were a regular nightmare, we were rushed so. Since the wedding things have been almost as busy. New Year's night we were shivareed and presented with a big box of candy. When we aren't out we are having company.

I hope you don't think Kaurin is in the army because he is a captain. He is a Master Mariner. I'll send some pictures of him as soon as I can get some.

We are living in the house which I had rented for the winter. It is a comfort to have someone to fix fires, take out the ashes, fill the lamps, shovel the walks and such things for me on school days. He even gets breakfast for me. I'd been going without and not having much lunch. I suppose I'll really start adding the pounds now!

I have a new scholar today which makes the enormous number of twelve students. He seems like a nice little chap; he's in the fifth grade.

It is not so very cold here now. We've had some awfully cold weather though. There is very little snow, only three or four inches. They say they never have very much here. We had a thaw and a south wind last week that blew the ice all out of the Bering Sea, but it is all back again now.

The days are getting much longer. At least it seems so. Of course, a few more minutes of daylight added on both morning and afternoon help a lot.

My Christmas program went off fairly well. It was forty-five minutes long which was pretty good for such a small school, I think. I received quite a few nice presents - slippers, stockings, step-ins, candy, ivory napkin rings, stationery, handkerchiefs, a pair of gloves, games, and a pin. Guess that's all. Now the wedding gifts are coming in. I have a silver pie knife, cold meat fork and a

cube-sugar tray.   Of course, it's impossible to buy
anything here.

Hope you are all well after the shock I've given you.
Will write again soon.

Lovingly, Marion

St. Michael, Alaska
January 28, 1924

Dear Mother,

Didn't have a letter from anyone in the last mail but
suppose everyone was waiting to hear from me. Mailed
you a package a couple of weeks ago. Hope you get it all
right.

I broke my watch last week so I am lost now. Won't
have it until spring I suppose. I have a watch that I use
in school but when I wind it, it sounds like a threshing
machine and ticks like an alarm clock.

We are having very nice weather; cold, of course,
but very bright and sunny. Have had very few cloudy
days so far this winter.

Well, I have been married four weeks today. It
doesn't seem that long. We got a wedding gift Saturday
of a case of oranges, a nice gift since we both like them
and use a lot and they are quite high here.

I opened my glass of jelly that I brought with me
from the farm a week ago for a dinner party. It tasted
so good. I also had a fruitcake from Bunker Hill, Illinois
that one of the girls I went to school with sent me for
Christmas.   I served baked ham, mashed potatoes,
carrots and peas, pear salad, hot rolls, coffee, jello and
cake. It was a good dinner - everything turned out good
for once. I'm having another dinner next Sunday, then
all my obligations will be paid.

We didn't have any lights on in school yesterday for

the first time since we started. We really could have used
them after half past three though.

Have a sore throat this morning. Guess I got it from
the school children. They are all coughing.

News is scarce so will close.

Love, Marion

St. Michael, Alaska
January 31, 1924

Dear Helen,

Your letter of December 9 came two weeks ago and
as usual I'm late in answering. I try to answer letters the
day they come or for the next week's mail but I find that
married life sort of interferes with getting my work done.
Husbands seem to require so much attention and Kaurin
seems to think I ought to spend my evenings entertaining
him. If I start work he starts the phonograph and puts
on some jazzy record and does a war dance around the
room with the cat for a partner. He raises such a
rumpus I can't work. It's gotten to the place when he
starts his performance the cat beats it under the table and
the dog asks to be let out.

Yes, I did have a nice Thanksgiving and Christmas
this year. I spent them with Kaurin, of course, and we
had dinner both holidays at the Williams'.

Kaurin will be away on the boat most of the summer
and maybe I'll go to Nome then. They have more
entertainment there, naturally.

We are having rather nice weather, cold but bright.
The days are getting so much longer and that seems so
good.

I am going to order some new clothes this spring and
I have seen a knicker suit that I really like. They are all
the vogue just now.

Will close with love to all the family, from

Marion

St. Michael, Alaska
February 18, 1924

Dear Mother,
Your letter of January 6 came last Friday and I was so glad to hear from you.

Yes, I imagine I did surprise a few people. Kaurin did too, I guess. We have received some really funny letters. No one on my side gets his name right. I guess it was the fault of the telegraph we sent. I got a letter from Council addressed to Mrs. Captain Olsen and Kaurin got a letter from a friend of his in South Dakota congratulating him and Mrs. Campbell.

I'm writing this during recess time and I wish you could see my boys playing rocking chair. They stand back to back by twos, lock arms and lift each other from the floor. They play football most of the time but it is too windy today. We have about one bad day a week.

The wind is from the north today and just goes right through the building. The stove doesn't seem to do any good. I'm bundled up in my sweater but I'm still cold. Just hate the idea of going home for lunch in the wind. I guess it isn't much below zero but the wind makes it seem much colder.

We are going to have to move in about three months; not sure just where but we have three places in mind. We haven't much to move, thankfully. We do own a teakettle and bread knife though. Oh yes, a can opener too - three essentials in this country!

Hope you are all well.

Lovingly, Marion

St. Michael, Alaska
March 7, 1924

Dear Helen,

Your letter of January 15 came two weeks ago and I just realized I hadn't answered it.

I am pretty sure you know by now that Kaurin is a captain on a boat, a small steamer; I guess she is really a tug. Don't think for one moment it is the *Leviathon* but there are worse boats on the river. He owned the boat until the day before I met him.

Well, we are going to have to move in May but still don't know just where. I am getting anxious to know but Kaurin doesn't seem to be very worried.

I think Alaska is a pretty good place to live. We both have good jobs and are saving money every month. Our expenses the first month we were married totalled about $250 but were much less for February. I guess between us we are making more money than anyone else in this town. I must admit though that we are far from rich.

I sent out for a knicker suit last week. Can't you just see me all dressed up in pants? I think I'll be on the boat quite a little this summer and knickers will be so much nicer than skirts.

Last night going home from school one of my little boys ran into me with his sled. He had one dog hitched to it and the tow line caught my ankles and upset me. I must have made a real picture. The poor child was scared to death and for some reason he kept yelling "Ouch!" Kaurin was watching (near hysterics) from the window and now he tells me that he's going to have to insist that I wear longer bloomers if I'm going to entertain the local population with my stunts.

Kaurin and I are both gaining weight. We eat enough to make us both tubs. Surprisingly enough to you, I suppose, I have everything there is to be had to cook with here and I'm getting better all the time. My bread has gotten so good that one baking won't last more than a week now.

Our cat, Hootch, is turning out to be lots of company. Kaurin tells me that he's a great talker, always complaining. He keeps him dressed up in some crazy thing all the time. He didn't like it at first but now he seems proud of his trimmings (of course the Eskimos think we are out of our minds). We put him out when we leave the house and at night so now when he sees us getting our overshoes or starting to undress, he hides; some wise cat.

The ice has gone so far out into the Bering Sea we can hardly see it today. It will probably be back tomorrow. I'm really enjoying this nice weather.

Kaurin, like most men, is never so happy as when tearing some old engine apart. That's what he is doing today; pulling an engine out of some old boat. He is working by the year and has other work to do besides boss. He really hasn't done much since the first of November but draw his salary so I guess a little work won't hurt him. I think he likes to be doing something though.

As usual news is scarce so will close for this time.

Lovingly, Marion

St. Michael, Alaska
March 31, 1924

Dear Mother,
Just a few lines to let you know we are well and getting along fine.

March is going out like a lion but I'm not sure about the proverbial lamb up here. It is snowing and blowing today but could be much colder than it is.

There hasn't been any mail for two weeks and we are all out of reading material. There was a snow slide or something on the railroad in southeastern Alaska which has put the mail behind. We have subscribed to nine papers and magazines but it looks like we won't get them for some time. We had so looked forward to some of them arriving this week.

Tomorrow is school election so I get a half day free since the election is held in the school house. Kaurin is to be one of the judges. I suppose there won't be but half a dozen votes cast.

We are going to move in eight weeks, the day after school is out. As soon as it is a little warmer I'll have my hands full as we will have to clean the place we are moving into. Kaurin is working now whenever the weather is good so I'll have most of it to do myself.

I have a new pupil today. She is only four years old and there is another one of the same age that will be starting as soon as the weather is good enough. I expect to have a grand time with them.

I don't know whether I told you that my engagement and wedding rings came two weeks ago. They are very pretty and the diamond is quite large. I am so proud of them.

Hope you are all well.

Love, Marion

Chapter VII

Home on the Bay

Marion arrived in Alaska with glowing ideas of gold mines, fur coats and wealth. We find her now a mature young wife. At this point she seems content with her cabin and good warm stove.

The ultimate in life now seems to be to own a Delco generating plant.

St. Michael, Alaska
April 9, 1924

Dear Mother,

We are having regular March weather, cold one day and almost hot the next (just like back home). It thawed quite a lot yesterday but I suppose it will snow tomorrow.

I have three new pupils now so I have all eight grades and three sections to my first grade. It makes for a busy life trying to keep ahead of all of them.

Kaurin bought our cabin last week and we are going to move in a couple of weeks now, just as soon as we can get it fixed up and cleaned. All the cupboards in the kitchen need a good cleaning and there are lots of them. The kitchen is much better than the one I have now. It is a double house and so quite large but I don't think we will use the upstairs except for storage. My dining and living room are all one but it is a large room. The furniture is just fair but we are happy to have it.

We have a fairly good round dining room table. There is a good carpet on the floor, a good stove, writing desk, fair book case and a side board which we will use for a bureau too. Kaurin has bought me a travelling phonograph, one of those little ones that folds up like a suitcase and I'll soon have a sewing machine too. And (praise be) there is even a nice porcelain bathtub in the house as well as a refrigerator. We are planning to have some ice put up and sure as we do it will be a cold summer and we won't need it.

Our new house is only about half a block from the school and close to Kaurin's work too. There are eight rooms all together but we will only use three since it would take too much fuel to heat it all. The other rooms will be fine for storage. It will be wonderful not having to store junk in the living room!

I've been making a dresser scarf and tonight I'll hem some dish towels. I've been saving up my flour sacks.

We sent out to Sears and Roebuck for a new set of dishes and a lot of kitchen utensils. I'm going to have one handy kitchen when we get through but sometimes it's hard to wait so long for things to come from the outside.

There are only six more weeks of school now. I will be glad when it is over; keeping house and teaching keeps me busier than I like.

We haven't had any mail for a month but I hope to have some this week. It's time we were getting some of our magazines.

Hope you are well. We are both fine.

Love, Marion

St. Michael, Alaska
April 14, 1924

Dear Mother,

Your letter of February 21 came Saturday and we were so glad to hear from you again.

It's been very cold here the past few days. I froze my nose yesterday, the first time this winter. We had been over to our new house and on the way home we both had our arms full of bundles of laundry and I couldn't cover my nose. When we got into the house the whole tip was white but it was just the skin fortunately.

I'm about as tired as I've ever been in my life. I've been washing, ironing, baking, cleaning and getting ready to move and Kaurin has been working hard too. He's blackened stoves, carried in wood, coal and ice, carried out rubbish and helped me with the cleaning too. I still have curtains to make and table linen to wash but I can do that after we move. I hire my bedclothes and heavy washing done but do all my own table linen. The Eskimos can't seem to iron to suit me.

I've been getting some interesting mail from the girls back home. One of them got so excited when she heard about my marriage that she leaned against the telephone and pulled the whole front off. She says she's coming to Alaska - all prepared with rings and trousseau. Another one wants me to find a sailor for her to write to. I guess she thinks they grow wild up here.

This is probably the last letter you will receive until the boats start running. This week's mail is perhaps the last over-land mail to go out.

Lovingly, Marion

St. Michael, Alaska
April 24, 1924

Dear Mother,

Got your letter last week and will answer right now since they tell me there is to be an outgoing mail this week.

It has been very cold and stormy lately. We had the worst storm of the winter last Saturday. Sunday night it was so cold that my plants froze - even the dirt they were in.

We moved to our own house Tuesday and it seems so good to have a place we can keep warm. The kitchen range keeps the whole place comfortable. We have a big hot water tank and it stays hot all night. Of course using only two rooms helps. We have it fixed up so cozy. I don't have the curtains up yet but I'm learning that I can't do everything at once.

I've been sick with the flu ever since last Friday. I manage to keep going but that is about all. Most of the children at school have been sick and I seem to catch everything they do.

Our magazines started coming last week so we expect

a large mail this week. The mail was held up so long with the snow slide that they are making special trips now.

I'm going to roast some beef for dinner tonight. I hardly know what to get for meals since it's so hard to find anything to cook these days. There's not much choice in foods right now.

Only six or eight weeks until the boats begin to come. We'll be glad to see them again.

Write soon.

Lovingly, Marion

St. Michael, Alaska
June 14, 1924

Dear Mother,

The *Vic* will be in today and as usual I have left my letters until the last minute. Of course mail goes every week now and it won't make as much difference.

I am well but Kaurin has a bad cold. He worked in the rain the other day and got soaking wet but couldn't leave the boat until eight at night as they were filling the oil tanks. The hard work will soon be over. He goes to work at four in the morning now.

I hardly know what to do with myself with school closed. I've been housecleaning but the days are so long that I get tired of working before the day is over. I'm doing my own washing now. I got tired of having my clothes come home smelling like fish and seal oil. Then too, the lady kept raising the price on me. We have running water in the house and hot water all the time so it isn't hard. We have all the coal I want to burn so the ironing isn't a problem either.

We are fixed very comfortably in our own house now and haven't suffered from the cold since we moved. We got our bathroom fixed up the other week so we can even soak ourselves in the tub now. Heavenly!

I am anxious for the *Vic* to get here. We should both have new clothes and a lot of new dishes on this ship.

The summer has been cold and rainy so far. It's been raining all morning and looks as if it will keep on. It put me in a baking mood and I have a ham and an apple pie fixed already.

The boats are coming in fast now. It is a beautiful sight. I have a good view of the bay from my front window and can see all that is going on.

The little boy from next door saw Kaurin put his arms around me the other day and he has made a tour of the neighborhood telling everybody that "Ole loves teacher" and proceeding to show them how. I understand that it was a pretty good show. I can just imagine.

Will end this letter and write again when I hear from you. Hope you are all well.

Love to all, Marion

St. Michael, Alaska
June 16, 1924

Dear Helen,

I think your letter of February 28 was the last one I received. We moved into our own home in April and some things aren't straight yet.

I don't really have any idea how long we will stay here. I suppose as long as Kaurin can keep this job, which pays fairly well, and we have a home we might as well stay. You know, sea captains aren't rich men unless they own their own boats and then it is a gamble. Kaurin makes enough so that we will always have plenty to eat and wear and a little to save besides, if he has no accident. We own our own home now too and though it is no mansion, I've seen much worse places up here. It is all wired for electric lights and Kaurin said last night that some day we will have a Delco plant. That's the last word in comfort for me.

We came close to being burned out a couple of weeks ago. The jail caught fire and there was a high wind and no water. Two other buildings caught but they managed to save them. The jail burned to the ground though. The ground all around here is soaked with crude oil and things looked bad for awhile. They had to keep men watching for a whole day after the fire since the soil here is just like peat.

Will close for this time.

Lovingly, Marion

St. Michael, Alaska
August 20, 1924

Dear Mother,

I haven't heard from any of you for several weeks but suppose you are all fine.

Kaurin's trip to Bethel was something less than a success. They were gone six days and were in a gale all of that time. They only got about two hundred miles from here and the barge sank. Of course the barge was all wood so that she stuck out of the water about two feet. They started back with her but the night before they got here the storm got so bad it took the house off. Oh yes, they lost about seven barrels of crude oil too. That barge was worth about thirty thousand when they left and about five thousand when they got back. Poor dears! That's enough to make a man lose his sense of humor.

The boat got in here early in the morning of the day we expected a message from them. Kaurin insists he thought my eyes would roll down my cheeks when I opened the door to find him standing there. I certainly felt as though they would. The whole thing was quite a <u>blow</u> to all of us (that's a pun!)

The weather is fairly warm but terribly wet. It rains every day at some time or another and I have to wear rubbers all the time. I sent for some new ones but they were too large so back they had to go. Shopping for the smallest things can be so inconvenient at times.

I'll call this enough for this time.

Lovingly, Marion

St. Michael, Alaska
September 8, 1924

Dear Helen:

Once more I am back on the job. Only eight have enrolled so far and most of them are small.

Not much news. Just happy routine. Our new puppy gets cuter every day and Hootch, our cat, isn't afraid of her any more. He just slaps her face if she gets too near.

I finally received my new brown tweed knicker suit. It's really quite classy, though I can't say that the same opinion is held by some of the Eskimo ladies.

We had lovely weather last week but now it is cold and rainy. I guess winter is here.

I do apologize for this short note but I just wanted to let you know that we are well and busy. I promise to write again soon.

Much love,

Marion

St. Michael, Alaska
October 16, 1924

Dear Helen:

I'm sorry I don't get more letters off to you but there just doesn't seem to be enough exciting things to write about.

This is my sixth week of teaching and no pay yet! We've been buying fuel for winter and are a little short just now too. Also, Kaurin is ready for a trip to Seattle and could have used a little cash. He is taking the *Meteor* out and was to have started last evening but a bad storm came up and they couldn't go. He may go only as far as Seward but even so he will be gone six weeks. If he goes to Seattle he won't be back until New Year's. He will return to Seward by steamer, from there to Nenana by railroad and then home either by dog team or on skis. As it is about 750 miles from Nenana to St. Michael and he can only average about thirty miles a day, it will take over three weeks from there with the best of luck. I hate to see him go; the trip is so dangerous. But, of course, it means quite a bit of money.

It has been snowing and is very cold here now. The thermometer was down to zero on the 12th, so you can see it is real wintery.

I'm glad you like Kaurin's looks. He is just as jolly as can be when he gets acquainted, but he is very bashful. I often wonder where he got the courage to propose to me. I shall miss him terribly while he is away.

'Bye for now.

Love, Marion

St. Michael, Alaska
October 28, 1924

Dear Mother,

I've been receiving letters from the girls about your operation. Sorry to hear you were under the weather but hope you will be well by the time you get this. I'm sure Jessie would tell me that anyone could recover from two major surgeries by that time. She doesn't think much of our mail service. She thought they were slow this summer but they will be even slower now. Actually, it's a wonder that they go as fast as they do. Can you imagine that these mails go the first thousand miles by dog team, and as they carry from five hundred pounds to a half ton they can't move very fast. Then there are storms to be considered too. In summer it takes the mail about two weeks to get up the river to Nenana, two days to Seward from Nenana on the railroad and a week from Seward to Seattle on the boat. I know it's slow but I'm happy for the service, such as it is.

School is going on in the same old fashion. Two months gone by and no pay in sight yet.

Everything was upset here for a while. They suddenly decided to take the *Meteor* outside for repairs and Kaurin was going along. They left here on Friday afternoon and got about two hundred miles away, then ran into a very bad storm. I guess they came close to seeing the bottom. The *Meteor* was covered with ice from top to bottom, about six inches thick. Something was wrong with the boiler and they ran short of fuel. I guess they had plenty but couldn't get at it for some reason so they turned around and came home. I must admit that I was happy to have him back so soon.

Since Kaurin got home (all frustrated), he has poured all his energy into fixing up the house. He has put castors on almost everything that moves and given everything in the house a coat of varnish (I'm glad the cat and dog kept out of his way).

Kaurin, Mollie the dog and I went on a picnic last Sunday. We took our lunch and scrambled up the beach a couple of miles, built a fire, melted ice, made coffee, ate and came home. Mollie ate most of our lunch, apples and all. As it was below zero we couldn't stay long in one place. Still, we were out three hours and I've been sleepy ever since. Can you imagine picnicking in zero weather - by choice?

Lovingly, Marion

St. Michael, Alaska
January 5, 1925

Dear Mother,

Just received word of Father's death. These are the times when it is almost unbearably hard for me to be so far away from all of my loved ones.

How I long to be with you to comfort you, but I am sure the girls and Leonard will care for your every need. This message grieves our hearts, Mother, but we must count this a blessing that his suffering is over.

My love and prayers,

Marion

St. Michael, Alaska
February 17, 1925

Dear Mother,

Received your letter from Mancelona and hope you are well. Kaurin and I have both been ill for the past two weeks. I missed a week of school but am back now. Kaurin still looks wretched but he is sawing wood today.

It's been so terribly cold, almost fifty below zero a couple of times, and we've used a lot of fuel. I froze my knees about a month ago when it was forty-five below.

They have had a diphtheria scare in Nome. I don't know for sure but I believe there were twenty-eight cases reported. There were five deaths before they got antitoxin and none since then, thank goodness.

I made an orange flavored gelatin with Knox's last night and it only took half an hour to set. I have finally found something this thirty below zero weather is good for! But it sure makes the wood and coal fly. I'll be glad to see the warmer weather come.

You wrote about getting a chicken from the farm. I wish I could. We got four to celebrate the Christmas holidays and what do you suppose they cost? Sixteen dollars! I nearly went up in smoke - and then I almost wished the chickens had. They were little bits of tough old things. I stewed one and had to cook it for four hours to get it tender enough to eat. We've just got some beef from Nome that was a fairly decent price - fifty- five cents a pound. We were so tired of the reindeer. In about two months we'll be getting ducks and geese again. I have several more letters to write so will close for now.

Love, Marion

Chapter VIII

TRANSPORTATION, COMPLIMENTS OF MOLLIE

There were no cars, no trucks, and no highways in North Alaska when Marion was there. Transportation was by wagon, boat, or dog sled. Because of Kaurin's occupation they were able to put their boat and motor to good use but their most practical means of transportation was their dog sled.

Building a sled and raising their own team was an enjoyable project for the Olsen family.

Meet Mollie's puppies.

St. Michael, Alaska
March 3, 1925

Dear Mother,
 Your letter came yesterday and it was good to hear from you, as usual.
 Yes, I am feeling fine again but Kaurin isn't over the grippe yet. He was feeling better until we went for a long walk Sunday - about seven miles, I guess. I suppose it was too much for him for the first walk after being so ill. It made me lame for Monday but I soon got over it.
 It is quite a bit warmer now, twenty or so above zero. I am so glad to see warm weather come for even a few days.
 Mollie had puppies a week ago today. She is only nine months old herself. She gave birth to six but only two lived. There was only one male in the bunch and he has survived so far. I don't know what Kaurin is going to do with the female. They are such a nuisance in a team. A good male will bring fifty dollars any day.
 Only nine more weeks of school. The kids are having recess now and chattering like magpies. These Eskimo children are such chatterers.
 I made noodles for supper last night and they turned out beautifully. You would have been proud of me if you had seen them.

Love to all, Marion

St. Michael, Alaska
March 20, 1925

Dear Helen,
 We have had terribly cold weather this winter. It's warmer now but we will probably have plenty of cold weather yet since April is usually a bad month here.

I wish I had some one with a good imagination to cook for me for a week or two. There is so little here to fix now. There are no apples left and there hasn't been any meat for most of the winter. We have to send to Nome for it and by the time it gets here it costs so much we feel like putting it in the safe. I think I'll turn into a weenie if I eat or see many more.

Work is sort of doubling up again now. Kaurin is working so I have to do a lot of things at home.

Our Christmas was kind of skinny this year. I ordered a jacket and bath robe through one of the stores for Kaurin but they didn't get here so I gave him socks, garters, arm bands, slippers and handkerchiefs. He gave me a box of candy, fountain pen, berry spoon and scissors.

It is starting to snow again. There has been more snow in the last week than we've had all winter. At least it seems that way.

You should see Mollie's puppies. They are too cute for anything. They walk around but aren't very steady yet and are so fat they roll. The cat, Hootch, doesn't like them at all.

This isn't a newsy letter but it's all I have to tell. There hasn't even been a party since New Year's, I guess.

Kaurin sends his best.

Lovingly, Marion

St. Michael, Alaska
June 21, 1925

Dear Helen,

The first *Vic* has come and gone and I never even saw her. So you can see that summer is really here.

The last three days have been warm and bright and it seems good, good, good! I have all the doors and windows open now.

I think Kaurin and I are going on a camping trip if the weather stays fine and the mosquitos don't eat us up. We have a little sail boat and an outboard motor so we can have all kinds of fun.

July 13, 1925

Sorry about this. I didn't get your letter finished and then we were away on a ten-day camping trip the last of June and the first of July. Had fine weather all the time, not one shower, and I got beautifully sunburned. We took our little boat and motor (our substitute for a car) and went about sixty miles up the Yukon River. The mosquitos got so thick then that we couldn't enjoy going any further so we came back and poked along the coast. We took a mattress and lots of canned stuff, slept in the boat and cooked our meals over a bonfire. It was lots of fun but it was good to get home and have a bath and sleep in a real bed.

I guess the rainy season has commenced. The days are growing shorter fast now.

Our neighbor's dog has eight puppies. She had twelve but they got rid of all the females. It's nice they don't feel the same about female people as they do about female dogs!

Write soon.

Lovingly, Marion

St. Michael, Alaska
September 4, 1925

Dear Mother,

The *Vic* is here again and as usual I am hurrying to get my letters done in time to make the boat.

I've been away from home for a week visiting a

nurse at Unalakleet. Mrs. Butler and I had heard so much about the town we wanted to see it.

Unalakleet is about the size of St. Michael but more desolate as no boats except the mail boat goes in there. The town is built on a sand spit so they can have wonderful gardens, including potatoes. This year was an exceptionally good year. They have beautiful flower gardens and raise wonderful sweet peas and pansies. It's really quite pretty.

Kaurin is running the *S.S. Donaldson* between here and Nome. I got here last night just in time to see him leave. They had a bad storm coming over from Nome and couldn't get the boat into Unalakleet so I came home on a trading boat. We had a fine trip both ways.

They painted the inside of the school house while I was gone, white walls and gray floor. White! Can you imagine?

It is so stormy today they can't unload freight. It started raining this morning; hope it clears soon so I can wash. Everything is full of water so for once I can use all I want. It has been so dry this summer that water has been scarce at times.

We are both well. Take care of yourself.

Love, Marion

St. Michael, Alaska
September 24, 1925

Dear Mother,

I suppose this will be the last mail by boat, so it will be some time before you get another letter.

Winter is here early. We had a very heavy snow storm the other day. It has melted in the town now but the mountains are still white.

We've had hard winds for several weeks and Kaurin

must be having bad weather now. He left yesterday morning at half past four for Nome, going by way of Unalakleet and Golovin. The wind came up soon after he left so I expect he is at Golovin. That is the only place with shelter for a boat. He can't unload at Nome with a south wind blowing so there is no use going on. It's almost impossible to make his runs on time now because of the weather. On the last trip it took twenty-four hours longer to get into St. Michael than he had expected and I had my nose in the window most of that time, watching. Believe me, that waiting is almost as melodramatic as it sounds.

Mollie has three of the cutest puppies. They aren't quite two weeks old so they haven't their eyes open yet. She had ten but there were only three males. They all look like her, white with brown ears.

The dogs are getting heavy coats early this year. Mollie is naturally long haired and has a terrible coat of wool now. I guess that's a good indication that we are going to have an early winter. The birds went south two weeks ago. There's no ptarmigan this year and, wouldn't you know, I have a twenty-two rifle coming in on this boat. Oh well, I don't suppose I'd have nerve enough to shoot a bird anyway.

We are also expecting a couple of hundred dollars worth of groceries on this boat. Can you imagine long-distance grocery shopping? I wish they would hurry and come. I hate to buy things that we have on our order because we send for better grade stuff and so much of everything. I am so hungry for boiled ham. I haven't had meat to eat for a week.

I am so sleepy. Seems as though I am up so early and to bed so late these days. I was ironing by five yesterday morning and was baking bread at two one night. They can't bake on the *Donaldson* so I have been making the crew some cookies and doughnuts for a treat. Next trip Kaurin wants a lemon pie. I can't imagine anything worse to try to take on a boat that just about turns over it rolls so. But I guess I could send lemon pudding and it will taste the same.

Hope to hear from you soon.

Love, Marion

St.Michael, Alaska
October 2, 1925

Dear Mother,

Kaurin has been gone over a week now and we've had word that he still hasn't reached Nome nor Golovin. I can't understand it. They must be on the beach or rocks somewhere. Yesterday was a fine day so it seems as though they should have shown up somewhere.

The *Vic* isn't here yet. She was very slow on the way up - too many storms, I guess.

My boss was here Monday all day. We didn't expect him and it made me very nervous to have a visitor all day. He was very nice though and didn't criticize anything I did. My scholars were real good, bless them.

The puppies are growing fast. They are walking around now and notice things, noises especially. Mr. Henderson said that if it hadn't been so far to Juneau he would have taken one home to his little girl. I wish he had. I can think of several things I'd rather have than three more dogs.

Love, Marion

P. S. Just got word from Kaurin. He had to beach the boat and walk to Golovin. He is all right and will be home soon, thank heaven!

St. Michael, Alaska
November 17, 1925

Dear Mother,

Winter seems to be here at last, although it isn't very cold right now. The bay is beginning to freeze - a month later than last year. The days are very short but I don't mind any more.

The school children are having the measles one after another but the States aren't making any fuss about us. One of my pupils is dying of tuberculosis. It's so sad.

I'm having a sewing bee; just finished making a dress out of that brown suit I bought the year I was home. It made into a fine warm dress and I even trimmed it with beaver fur. I'm using it for school as it doesn't wrinkle or show dirt and I can wash it.

The dogs are all howling to be hitched up and the kids are all blowing their noses so it's really quiet in here - the kind of quiet I usually have during recess.

Kaurin is having a dog sled made but I think he will have to push it himself. The pups won't be large enough to use this winter even if we're able to raise them.

There is only one mule left on the island now and he is being used for hauling coal. They just upset a load outside of the school window. There is a deaf mute Eskimo driving the mule and the men have taught him to say "gee" and "haw." So he drives with a stick - so many raps mean "gee" and so many for "haw" and, I guess, for "whoa." He's quite an interesting character - can read, write, and talk on his fingers but he uses signs all the time. He's quite a favorite around here.

The mailman has had to carry the mail on his back so far this year. His trip is about sixty miles over tundra. Some hike, a hundred and twenty miles a week. I'd call him a real _male_ man, wouldn't you? We could see a fire across the bay last night so I guess he was waiting for daylight to cross as the ice is not very strong yet.

Haven't heard from any of you for a long time. Hope to soon.

Lovingly, Marion

St. Michael, Alaska
December 1, 1925

Dear Mother,

Here it is almost Christmas time and I haven't a present ready for anyone. I don't know where all the time goes.

Kaurin has been breaking Mollie in to drive. She learned in one lesson of half an hour. We had an idea that it would be impossible to teach her as pet dogs are usually no good for driving. So we're very proud of her. She helps haul ice now and will be good to break the pups in when they are old enough.

Kaurin is putting up ice for next summer. Last year we didn't have any and water was scarce for weeks.

There's another new baby in town. They are arriving thick and fast now. There will be yet another one in March so it looks like I can keep my job.

I know this is short but I will write after the holidays when I have things to write about.

Love, Marion

St. Michael, Alaska
January 26, 1926

Dear Mother,

Sorry it has been so long since I've written. I intended to write during Christmas vacation but I was rather busy. The children gave their program Christmas Eve and there was so much to do before that.

We had a nice tree and every one got lots of presents. I got five boxes of candy, a pair of pink garters, a glass dish, a silk handbag, collar and cuff set, piece of linen for a dress, some carved ivory, a whisk broom holder and some handkerchiefs.

We went to the Evans' for Christmas dinner. Just before New Year's, Mrs. Butler had a turkey dinner and on New Year's Eve we had our turkey dinner for our anniversary. We had a twenty-two pound turkey and it took two loaves of bread to stuff it. Kaurin gave me a pair of sterling silver candlesticks and a casserole in a silver frame for Christmas so I had the table lighted with candles. Very festive. It was fun to fix but - do you have any recipes for left-over turkey?

Kaurin has finally broken the pups to drive. They are good but look funny because they are so small. Mollie thinks it is great fun to be hitched up with them.

The days are growing much longer. We didn't even have to have a light in school this morning. This has been such a mild winter. We'll probably have plenty of cold weather yet though. Thankfully it hasn't frozen in our house this winter even though the fires usually go out before morning. Our wood seems to be holding out much better this winter.

Kaurin and I are well and hope you are too.

                                                    Love, Marion

St. Michael, Alaska
February 3, 1926

Dear Helen,

The old groundhog saw his shadow yesterday so it's six more weeks of winter for us. We would have it anyway, I'm sure. The weather prophets say no summer for us because of a sun spot but we certainly are having a dandy winter.

Kaurin took me for a three-mile dog sled ride last Sunday. It was really a fine day. The pups are so small they're comical but they work like old dogs. When we stop they get all mixed up because they want to turn around and look at us.

It's beginning to seem like spring now. I'm making my orders up to send out so they will come in on the first boat. Present plans call for lots of new clothes. How do you like everfast gingham? I'm thinking of getting some.

This is short, of course, but it's almost noon and I feel hungry. I have one good appetite these days.

Love, Marion

St. Michael, Alaska
February 11, 1926

Dear Mother,

Your letter of January 4 came yesterday and I was happy to get such a long newsy one.

We have had a very mild winter. There are some bad storms now but they don't last long and the middle of the day is warm. It sets me thinking about spring housecleaning.

We are having great fun with the dogs these days. The pups are fine ones (I guess we are dog crazy). The cat is fat as a pig. I swear he's eaten half a reindeer this winter, about fifty pounds. Don't you think he ought to be fat?

We are having boiled beans for supper. We have them quite often since they are easy to fix. We never bake them up here for some reason.

My tubercular pupil has recovered some and is in

school again. He is very frail though. So many of the natives seem to have T.B.

Jessie sent me a very pretty pair of gloves for Christmas. They arrived yesterday. I needed them badly.

Love, Marion

Chapter IX

Baby Kaurin - Joy and Sorrow

1926   - The year of the crash for Marion and Kaurin. Their bank in the States closed and left them nearly penniless for the next few years. But they were young and strong enough to begin again.

This year also brought them a son - something to make a new beginning worthwhile.

St. Michael, Alaska
June 1, 1926

Dear Mother,

If my letters seem a little far between, it's because postage stamps are a little hard to come by lately. You probably heard that the bank where Kaurin and I had all our savings collapsed and it looks as though we won't be getting much of it back. Once in a while they send us a few dollars. It always seems to come just at the time when we are right down to nothing at all.

I have an announcement to make which should make you very happy. You are about to become a grandmother again. We are expecting an addition to our home in October. Kaurin and I are very happy but I am a little concerned because I won't be able to teach this fall. It will be up to Kaurin to keep us going for a while.

The new teacher will be coming in September. It will seem odd not to be teaching for the next year.

Give the news to all.

Love, Marion

St. Michael, Alaska
August 28, 1926

Dear Mother,

Guess it is about time for me to write again. The *Vic* will soon be here on her third trip. That means the summer is nearly over.

We've had a hot, dry summer and the scarcity of water has been terrible until the last ten days. Everyone has had to go across the bay, five miles away, to get water. We had to go at low tide for the spring is covered with salt water at high tide. Even at low tide we had to be careful or the water was brackish.

Kaurin is painting the house. He started several days ago and got the front painted and I guess that started the rain. The wind is blowing hard now but he says he has to paint while the sun shines, wind or no wind. When it rains he works inside. We are fixing a new bedroom for ourselves as I am apt to have the new teacher to room and board this winter if she wants to board instead of rent a house.

Kaurin was working on his gas engine in the dog house the other day and was almost gassed. Had the doors open too. He says he feels all right now but he doesn't look too skookum. He tells me he had his own party and it turned into a real gasser!

Must close.

Love to all, Marion

St. Michael, Alaska
October 15, 1926

Dear Mother,
Just a note to let you know that your new grandson is here. He was born October 13 and is a fine, healthy boy.

We have named him Kaurin Campbell Olsen. That should keep everyone happy on both sides of the family.

Love, Marion

St. Michael, Alaska
April 25, 1927

Dear Mother,
Your letter of March 14 came yesterday and I was so glad to hear all the news from home.

Instead of mud we are wading in snow this spring. More snow has fallen in the last two weeks than all the rest of the winter together and the break-up appears to be a long way off.

I think children stand a better chance up here than in the States. Baby Kaurin has had the sniffles a couple of times but otherwise he is fine. He has a nap out of doors every day; maybe that helps. Yesterday he weighed eighteen pounds, two ounces and he can sit alone and almost stand alone. He has no teeth yet but children up here always seem to be slow in getting them for some reason. He is just a darling, of course, and we love him dearly.

Glad to hear you are getting some new clothes. I am kept busy making baby dresses since he is growing so fast. Besides, housedresses seem to be my most important clothes these days.

Must run. Little Kaurin just woke up from his nap and I better go warm his mush (that's his food, not something we yell at the dogs!)

Love, Marion

St. Michael, Alaska
June 5, 1927

Dear Mother,
How are you? We are all fine now. Kaurin had a rather bad experience a couple of weeks ago but is all right now. It all happened on a trip to the Yukon.

Bob Johnson has the contract for putting the light houses along St. Michael Island and the coast of the Yukon River this year. It is ninety miles from St. Michael to the mouth of the Yukon. There is a natural canal separating St. Michael from the mainland that is used by the stern wheelers as they are shallow draft. Bob has a boat but no motor and we have a boat and motor, a tiny outboard motor of 1 HP or less. Since it takes two boats to hold the tanks of gas, Bob hired Kaurin to help. He was to furnish everything and pay Kaurin $50.

I knew Kaurin was to make the trip but not exactly when since the whole thing depended on wind and tide. Daylight doesn't matter as it is daylight all the time. Along about three o'clock one afternoon Kaurin said they were leaving. I wanted him to take some food along but no, Bob was to furnish it (Kaurin had more faith in Bob than I did). They were to be gone about three days. Three days came and went but their not being back wasn't surprising. But when eight, then nine days went by, I began to stew. I had made up my mind that if they weren't back the next day I was going to ask the Coast Guard at Nome to look for them.

At five a.m. of the tenth day, Kaurin came into the bedroom and asked if I had any food in the house. The canal is about thirty miles long and just about at the end of the canal, the motor had quit. He had rowed the rest of the way - about sixty miles. He had head winds most of the way and the sail was of no use. Then he rowed the ninety miles home and had no food except what he had eaten at Tom Backlund's place at the mouth of the Yukon. Bob had taken along six hardtack and some coffee, had run out of smoking tobacco and used the coffee in his pipe.

Poor Kaurin. He was one tired, hungry man. He just ate little dabs of food every hour or so that first day. He is fine now and back to work. Just one more frightening experience to add to a growing collection.

Baby Kaurin and I are fine. Will write again soon.

Lovingly, Marion

St. Michael, Alaska
December 5, 1927

Dear Mother,
 Your kind letter of October 12 came a week ago. I
have been going to write for a long time but just haven't
seemed able to get to it. I was rather busy before Baby
Kaurin was taken sick and of course afterward it was
hard to settle down to writing.
 Kaurin had finished work and been home about four
days before baby became sick. Just what it was caused
from we still don't know. He had colitis but it must have
been more than that. Mrs. Evans was afraid of
appendicitis but it didn't seem to be that. All baby
sickness seems so much alike. Sunday, October 2, he
slept too much, four hours in the morning and three
hours in the afternoon, and was a trifle cross. But as he
was teething I didn't think much of that, though I didn't
like his sleepiness. Monday morning he got up as usual,
ate his breakfast and played until nine when he became
a little cross. I thought he was tired so started to give
him his bath. Just after I put him in the water he
became blue and stiff, then white and limp. I took him
out and dressed him at once and wrapped him in a
blanket and put him to bed. He slept at once but woke
in a few minutes and cried. I was watching him as I was
so worried. He slept again, then woke and vomited. I
fixed him up and although he seemed weak he was better
for a few minutes. Then he started sleeping and waking
every few minutes, evidently in terrible pain.
 At noon he seemed so much worse I sent Kaurin for
Mrs. Evans. She thought it was probably just stomach
ache but gave him some medicine to relieve the pain. By
evening he seemed much better and slept well all night.
In the morning I gave him a little milk but he couldn't
retain anything. I tried several things but he just
couldn't keep anything down. By that time we knew he

had colitis but Mrs. Evans didn't seem worried. She said to keep him on a liquid diet for a week or so but that he should be better in a day or two. Wednesday afternoon he became worse and was in such terrible pain I couldn't hold him. Mrs. Evans tried to ease him but the medicine didn't seem to affect the pain at all. About eleven that night he began to vomit a black, tar-like substance. He was delirious and terribly restless. When Mrs. Evans came in the morning she was very worried. She thought it looked like digested blood but wasn't sure. She sent for one of the other women who is a nurse, but she seemed to know even less than the rest of us. At eleven we started giving him mineral oil; at two he seemed better and had no temperature but by six he had a temperature of 108 degrees. Mrs. Evans worked over him until one-thirty when she had his temperature down to 103. She is over fifty and was tired so went home and I took care of him. She told me how to tell when his heart began to fail. By nine the next morning he was conscious but all of a sudden his fingers, toes, nose and mouth became blue. We sent for Mrs. Evans but when she arrived he seemed better; he had some color and he was warm.   She did all she could to make him comfortable.

I had him trained and when he was conscious he insisted on being taken up. I'm sure moving and lifting him wasn't good when he was so weak. We gave him raw egg and toast and water and it seemed to quiet him. I even slept a couple of hours because I thought him better. At eleven he went into a coma but I thought he was asleep. At two I sent Kaurin to bed, he was so tired. At three thirty baby's breathing became irregular but I was too dumb to know what it meant. I had never seen death and didn't know what to look for. At four he passed away. I still believed I could feel his pulse and breath but when I called Kaurin he could tell at once that baby was gone.

Mrs. Evans says that if he had lived after that high temperature his heart and mind would not have been right so I suppose we shouldn't wish him back to suffer. But we do miss him so. He would have been walking in a few weeks and already knew a few words. He was a little mischief and kept me busy picking up after him. I thought I was taking good care of him but I must not have been doing the right things. This is so hard!

Kaurin misses baby terribly and can't talk of him yet. He was so proud of him and baby would mind his daddy when he wouldn't pay any attention to me.

It is two o'clock and getting dark so will close and take this to the post office.

Love, Marion

St. Michael, Alaska
December 13, 1927

Dear Helen,
Your kind letter came last week. Thanks ever so much.

We really do not know what caused baby's death. He was sick only five days. We think it was some digestive trouble but it is so hard to tell with a baby.

There doesn't seem to be much chance of our leaving here for some time. We are too hard up and this is an easier place than the States for poor people to live.

Mother says Henry isn't feeling well. I'm sorry to hear it. Tell him I said everything will be all right if he eats oatmeal mush every day, spinach every other day and raisins all the time and wears red flannel undies in winter time.

Kaurin is building a full-rigged ship model, twenty-five inches high and twenty-six long. It will be a beauty when finished but is a long job. We try to keep our time filled. The house seems so empty without baby to care for.

We have lots of snow these days; more now than ever before at this time of year. It isn't very cold today but it just keeps snowing.

I don't go out much and when I do I get terribly cold. I froze several toes last week.

Hope I'll hear from you again soon.

Lovingly, Marion

St. Michael, Alaska
December 28, 1927

Dear Mother,

Your letter of November 15 arrived yesterday. You should have mine before now. The packages haven't arrived yet but am sure they will soon and thanks ever so much to you and Helen. I'm sure we will like whatever it is.

How did Santa treat you? He was pretty nice to us. I received gifts too numerous to mention but want to tell you what Kaurin gave me. There were new overshoes, a black satin hat, a Victor record and a new wrist watch. I gave him several things, including a barometer which he has wanted for a long time.

Let me know if you have a good way to gain weight. I'm all angles and sharp bones.

We've been having cold, windy weather but it is nicer today. I'm getting ready for our New Year's dinner. Wish I could think of something new to have.

Love, Marion

St. Michael, Alaska
January 20, 1928

Dear Mother,
   Our Christmas packages came yesterday and we both
thank you. Kaurin was very pleased with his tie and also
the case it was in.
   I was afraid the packages had gone down with the
Northwestern which sank the tenth of December. They
saved the first class and the registered mail but that was
all, so I guess we will miss some of the magazines.
   It is quite nice today so Kaurin took me for a dog
sled ride. It was so soon after breakfast that Kaurin
didn't feel like running so we didn't go far. With only
four dogs we can't both ride all the time and Kaurin
won't let me run, so he has to do it all.
   We've had some terribly cold weather lately. Sunday
we went for a walk and I froze my right calf from my
overshoe top to my knee. That's the second freeze for me
this winter. We have more snow this winter than ever
before. Should make a good mining year next year.
Hope so anyhow.
   Thanks again for the lovely presents.

                              Lovingly to all, Marion

St. Michael, Alaska
February 24, 1928

Dear Mother,
   Your nice long letter came a week ago. As always,
we were glad to hear from you.
   We are having lovely weather now but we've had our
share of winter all right, and of course will get more.
We get out with the dogs once in a while.
   Neither one of us has so terribly much to do these

days. Kaurin was guard at the jail for a couple of weeks and I was on the jury one day. The poor fellow on trial was crazy and the whole thing was a joke. We could hardly keep our faces straight. In April I will be on the election board for a day and just now I am doing some work for one of the stores. Between times I do a little sewing. My ambition doesn't hold out for long at a time. I wish the snow would go so I could start gardening.

Mrs. Evans, Mrs. Butler, Mrs. Warren, and Mrs. and Miss Given all leave here on the first boat. I'm the only one staying home this summer.

There never seems to be any news. We can't take off and go places the way you can. Maybe later there will be more to write about.

Love, Marion

St. Michael, Alaska
April 12, 1928

Dear Helen,

I was very glad to get your long letter of February 24. I know I can't write such a long one.

Our days are very much the same. Kaurin is busy at the store from six in the morning until nine at night. He's home about fifteen minutes three times a day for his meals so I sit home and read and sew. Oh, how I miss baby.

I'm feeling fine most of the time now; at least I am able to eat better and am putting on some weight for the first time since little Kaurin left us.

Some friends in Chicago have a daughter that wants to come to Alaska to teach but I am not encouraging her. She seems so young. Miss Givin will stay here another year. I guess the $1,710 looks good to her. Wish I had taken the school last year when they offered it to me.

The enclosed pictures of Baby Kaurin are for you and mother to divide if you wish. It's rather late to be sending them but some of them I just had developed - and of course he is on my mind constantly. He would have been walking and talking long before this. The last time he was conscious he recognized Kaurin and said "Daddy."

It is warm today. One of my geraniums is budded so I guess spring will be here some time.

Love, Marion

Chapter X

Baby Francis Brings a Visit From Jessie

On June 21, 1928, the Olsen's second child arrived. Marion's sister Jessie came from the States for a visit and to help care for the new baby.

After the tragic experience with Baby Kaurin, the Olsens were naturally nervous about the health of their second child. On one occasion when he ran a fever, they hurried him by dog sled, wagon, and plane to Nome, only to find that the fever had disappeared and they had a healthy, happy baby.

St. Michael, Alaska
June 27, 1928

Dear Mother,

Jessie arrived from the States just the day before our new baby boy arrived. We have named him Francis Kaurin Campbell Olsen. He is a cute little thing and weighs seven pounds, eight ounces. It seems so good to have Jessie here to show him off to and to help me care for him. I feel a bit inadequate with him.

I guess Jessie had quite an experience on her trip. When they arrived at Nome they discovered eight cases of small pox on board the *Victoria*. The government doctors went on board ship and vaccinated all that needed it. Jessie was one of those that received the shot but thankfully she did not get sick. All the sick ones were Eskimos. She had to stay on board until they lifted the quarantine though.

Jessie saw some whales on the way over but was most impressed by the twenty-four hour daylight that we have here.

This is all for now. Will write later.

Love, Marion

St. Michael, Alaska
September 17, 1928

Dear Mother,

I guess you think that it is about time I write again! I haven't lacked the time but the ambition. Jessie and I sit and rock and talk. She will be leaving soon now and I know I am going to be very lonesome without her. Kaurin has one more trip up the river after the *Vic* leaves here so I will be alone for a time.

This summer has been horrid weather-wise. It has

been rainy ever since Jessie came. She sits on top of the stove and shivers. Actually, it is the first summer since I've been up here that we've used the heater. I don't mind it but of course I'm acclimated.

Baby Francis is fine. I suppose Jessie has told you all about him in her letters. He weighs eleven pounds, two ounces now. He cried quite a bit at first but is good now. He is rather spoiled as Jessie doesn't like to hear him cry and thinks he should be picked up. I guess Kaurin has bragged all along the river of how well the baby sleeps nights. It seems wonderful to have a baby in the house again.

It snowed a few days ago so Jessie is seeing the beginning of our winter. Berries are scarce this year so we couldn't treat her to those in a big way but we did have a few blueberries.

We expect the *Vic* any day now. I guess she is in Nome. I am so in hopes I can go out to her when Jessie leaves. Miss Given is to be married to the wireless operator as soon as she gets to St. Michael so we are looking forward to a wedding this fall.

Love, Marion

St. Michael, Alaska
October 5, 1928

Dear Mother,

Your letter of August 29 came some time ago. I suppose by the time you get this, Jessie will have been home for some time. We so enjoyed her visit. I wish you could have come with her. Kaurin didn't see her very much as he was away most of the time but she made a hit with him all right. It was wonderful for me to have her here but it seems so lonesome now. I don't know how we would have managed if she hadn't been here when

Francis was born. She didn't think much of St. Michael though.

Francis is a much smaller and more delicate baby than Kaurin was. He is so thin and white. Mrs. Evans prescribed cod liver oil and we think he looks better already. He was very fretful for a time but acts better now. Kaurin was quite a bit heavier at three months. It keeps me in a perpetual state of worry now I know he isn't right. He is a darling though and a very pretty baby.

I wish I had some of your home-canned fruit. This factory-canned fruit doesn't taste much like yours. I can't buy fruit to can up here for they charge too much. Plums are thirty-five cents a pound and peaches are fifty cents a pound.

We have had such a miserable summer, so rainy and cold. It has been clear for several days now but freezing cold.

It's nine p.m. and Kaurin has just brought the *Ensee* up to the dock. She looked like a Christmas tree with her red, white and green lights and her big search light playing all over the dock. They have been back for two days but he has to stay on the boat until they put her up for the winter. They can't do that just now as the tides are too low. I'll be glad to have him home again. I'm tired of building fires, taking out ashes and feeding dogs. Besides, I kind of miss him when he's away.

Baby is awake and crying so I guess I'd best see to him. He most likely is asking for dry pants. Wouldn't it be nice if you never had to change 'em or wash diapers?

Write often.

Love, Marion

St. Michael, Alaska
October 15, 1928

Dear Helen,

Jessie has been gone for three weeks now and it seems strange without her. We had such a good visit.

Kaurin has been home about a week and is busy getting the house ready for winter. There are so many things - storm windows, fixing the stoves and stovepipes, getting fuel, etc. He bought an old steamboat to tear down for fuel and that should keep him busy for a while. He really has plenty of work laid out to last him the winter.

Our grocery order didn't come this year for some reason. I suppose the order didn't get out on time. So we will have to economize again this year. Kaurin says to tell you that every winter is a hard winter here.

Francis isn't gaining as fast as he should but looks some better. He spit his cod liver oil into my face the other day. He has a nice aim! I've started putting orange juice in it since and it seems to go down a little better. Little Kaurin would take anything from a spoon but not this fellow.

Must rush this to the post office. Bye for now.

Love, Marion

St. Michael, Alaska
December 9, 1928

Dear Helen,

I think I owe you answers to two letters. I have let my correspondence go badly this year. Now there's a New Year's resolution for me!

I don't have much to write about. Kaurin has been busy cutting ice and doing the work on the house that I wrote you about. He's still cutting wood most of the time, trying to get enough together to last through the winter and next summer too.

The small pox or chicken pox, whichever it is, is raging. The doctors disagree of course. Some cases they call one and some the other. Very few have died so far so if it is small pox it is a light form. However, I am not taking any unnecessary chances.

Francis is not doing too well and we hardly know what to do. He has not gained for two weeks and last week he lost weight. He has very poor circulation and sometimes is as blue as if he had been painted. I can't tell you how worried I am.

We are having a very wintery winter. I haven't been out of the house since Thanksgiving.

Give my best to everyone and I'll write to mother next week. I suppose I'll just have to say the same things over again as there isn't anything going on.

Love, Marion

St. Michael, Alaska
February 6, 1929

Dear Mother,

Your letter of December 23 was a long time on the way as it arrived here only yesterday. Some kind of contract has been made with the aeroplane to deliver our mail at Unalakleet and it's the bunk. They can't travel in stormy weather so they just leave our mail any place and it takes ages to get back.

I am sorry to hear that you are not feeling well but hope by the time this reaches you, all will be well. We are all fine; even Francis for a change. There has been the biggest change in that baby the last three weeks! He has fleshed up and gotten good natured and even sleeps well at night. It sure seems good. I now have him on a combination of Eagle brand milk, evaporated milk and gruel and it works like a charm. He is still nervous but not nearly so afraid of people and is even able to sit up some. He also takes his orange juice and tomato juice and even his cod liver oil. Just now he is sleeping out of doors in the sun. It is quite a relief to see him look so well.

We have been having very mild weather recently - getting ready for a cold summer, I suppose. It does seem good to have our long days again.

Kaurin keeps busy on his wood pile. He has the shed nearly full for next summer. Our dogs have earned their keep for once, hauling all that wood to the shed.

I wish I could have been there for Jessie's wedding. I have missed out on them all. I suppose if it had been possible I would have missed my own.

In answer to your question, no, we don't have to work a pump handle but water and ice have to be carried in. I do have a sink though so I don't have to carry the water out. That may seem like a small thing to you but it's heaven to me! Jessie probably told you about our bathroom facilities. I have been away from such things for so long I wouldn't know how to make use of them (I'd sure like the opportunity to learn again though).

We did not do much for Christmas this year. Mr. and Mrs. Hoelscher had everyone for dinner and I had my usual New Year's dinner. It is always good food and fellowship.

Francis is waking up so I must close and get him something to eat. He drinks his milk from a glass and is quite a curiosity to most people.

Hope you find time to write again soon.

Lovingly, Marion

St. Michael, Alaska
September 16, 1929

Dear Mother,

Your letter came about two weeks ago and I was so glad to hear that you were having a nice time on the farm. I'd make a rotten farmer. I never even get around to weeding my lettuce bed. Now I have to dig among the chick weed to find the lettuce but the shade makes it white and tender (that eases my conscience). Wish I could have one of Jessie's tomatoes to go with it.

It sounds as though you've had some real storms there. I am glad we don't have cyclones here but we do have some terrible wind storms. The last bad one we had tore the roof off the dog house.

I've been quite busy this summer what with roomers, boarders and baking. I've made so many cakes I feel as though I look like one. Kaurin says that's not so but that I act like a smart cookie to him. Just at present I have one three-meal-a-day boarder and until last week I had a roomer for a while. One night I had six extras for supper. I didn't know about them until late in the afternoon so it meant a lot of last minute work. I charge a dollar a meal for transients, seventy five dollars a month for a steady roomer and boarder and four dollars a day if they stay only a few days. That looks like a lot but prices are high. Potatoes are eight pounds for a dollar and flour is the same.

Francis has been walking for three weeks now. He weighs twenty-five pounds, is quite tall and says a few more words now. Any noise outside, no matter what, is "dogs, dogs." He and Daddy have quite a time together.

The *Victoria* will be here in a day or two on her last trip of the season. The *Ensee* will make one more trip up-river and the season will be over. Then we will just settle in for the winter.

So far the weather is quite warm, a little rainy but

nothing like last summer. My pansies are still blooming nicely out of doors and some nasturtiums.

They have been killing reindeer here for the last two weeks to ship outside, but they aren't very fat and so not very good. We had some ducks the other day but after I cleaned them I couldn't seem to enjoy eating them.

Wish you could come spend a few weeks with me.

Love, Marion

St. Michael, Alaska
September 20, 1929

Dear Helen,

It has been a long time since I had a letter from you but probably longer yet since I have written. There seems to be so little to write about as we do about the same things every day. I have been busy with my boarders this summer but I think the last one has gone. He was here two weeks. Now I can do something else besides cook and wash dishes and table linen.

Kaurin is here now but will leave soon for his last trip up-river. When he comes home the *Ensee* will be beached and we will "beach" ourselves for the winter. Kaurin expects to build two row boats this winter. The lumber should be on this *Vic*.

I do wish you could see Francis. He is as cute as can be. Every time I take him anywhere he begs for something to eat. (It's most embarrassing). He calls the mule a dog. He used to call him Hootch. Now he calls anything that's furry Hootch. He is into everything at this age. I have to keep all the cupboards tied shut with string. Kaurin put hooks on them but he can open them as nice as can be. We think that's very smart of him, of course, but it doesn't make me too happy.

We have had a number of thunder and lightning

storms this summer. Then we all went around suffering with the heat. We really have had quite a nice summer though and no frost yet, which is unusual. I am still using lettuce from my garden.

The *Vic* is here and I am anxious for the mail. I'd better hurry my letters down to be sure and get them in the mail on time.

Francis sends a hug.

Lovingly, Marion

St. Michael, Alaska
January 1, 1930

Dear Mother,

I know it has been ages since I've written but I've told myself everyday that I would write "tomorrow." It seems to me I'm always busy at something. But Kaurin is doing the dishes for me tonight so I can write.

I haven't much pep today as I fixed a New Year's dinner for thirteen yesterday and we were up so late the night before. Francis is tired too but I have to wait for Kaurin to finish the dishes so I can give him his bath and get him to bed.

Francis was quite sick the first part of October but is surely healthy now. He doesn't remind us much of what he looked like a year ago. He talks quite a little now and picks up a new word every few days. He climbs everywhere, even goes up the stairs and they are like a ladder.

After Francis was sick I had an attack of acute indigestion. I got up to walk the floor in pain during the night and Kaurin found me unconscious on the couch. It must have been a while before he found me because I was ice cold. I was pretty sick for a few days but am fine now. Illness is always rather frightening way up here.

Until a week ago we have had a very mild winter. The bay in front of our house has just frozen over. It made the getting and sending of mail rather difficult as it all gets wet.

The days are so short I never seem to get my work done. I still have occasional boarders. Have to plan a dinner party for five tomorrow (dinner party! Doesn't that sound classy? Our wilderness is close to becoming civilized). I don't know what I'll serve for meat - maybe reindeer. We had our turkey last night. Kaurin always helps me when I have a crowd and I appreciate that very much. We have been married six years now.

I intended to get a package started to you and Helen weeks ago but didn't so will try to get it off in time for your birthdays.

I will answer Helen's letter soon. Her stove sounds glorious. Wish I had one like it. I have to shovel coal and wood into mine.

Love to all, Marion

Chapter XI

The Business Woman

When Marion first arrived in Alaska she bragged about not having to do her own janitorial work. Now, ten years later, a mature, hard working Marion is emerging. We find her teaching, cleaning and painting the school house and going into business as a cook, waitress, chambermaid, dishwasher, janitor and chore-girl in a hotel and restaurant.

St. Michael, Alaska
April 10, 1930

Dear Mother and Helen,

I think every week that I will write and something always happens. So now I am going to let everything else go and just do it. After the first of May we won't be able to send any mail until the boats begin running.

The winter was so late in starting I expect we will have a late spring. They wanted to begin repairing boats and barges in March but haven't been able to start yet. Kaurin is doing some carpenter work at Hoelscher's while he is waiting.

I am trying to get my sewing finished this month. I plan to run the hotel and restaurant this summer and must have the building ready the first of June. Wish you could come and take care of Francis for me. Kaurin looks worried every time the hotel is mentioned but never says a word. I know he is wondering how I will manage. I suppose I will have an Eskimo to help part of the time. Hope there are lots of travelers so I'll make a few dollars for my work. Some think the gold strike at Ruby will bring people through here but Kaurin and Capt. Hoelscher say not. I think they probably can guess as well as anyone for they know the river.

Francis is at the age where he loves to puddle in water and I caught him just now at the sink drinking soapy water with a toy cup. He washed his hands and then drank. Ugh (good physic, I guess). He is growing like a weed and talks quite a bit. The aeroplane has been here several times this spring and stopped in front of our house on the bay. He called it a bug.

Well, he has himself well soaked by now so guess I'd better give him a full bath and put him into dry things.

Lots of love from all of us,

Marion

St. Michael, Alaska
May 2, 1930

Dear Mother,

If I don't answer your letter that came yesterday, I don't know when I will get one out. Next week's mail will be the last to leave here until the boats start running again in the spring.

Kaurin has been working for some time. Only one more month and the boats should be launched. My job at the hotel and restaurant will be as cook, waitress, chambermaid, dishwasher, janitor and choregirl, all in one. The hotel is just a big old house and hasn't enough bedrooms but I thought I could rent the two extra ones at our house if I need to. It is going to mean a lot of work to get the hotel ready to open by the first of June. I'll be pretty busy from now on.

There is a chance that I will have a government job next winter. It will be either about twelve miles from here or north at a place called Teller. Nothing is settled yet, however.

I am busy sewing clothes for all of us. I also want to make a rug. I think I have enough old pink materials to make it all pink. I just long for something dainty and feminine-looking.

I was on the election board Tuesday and had to keep Francis there with me all the time, but he was as good as could be. He missed his nap but never fussed. He sure was tired when he got home though.

The news from home makes me afraid to come to the States for fear we will starve to death. It seems to be harder to get work there than here. We never expect to work more than six months out of the year up here so always try to be prepared for the other six.

Francis wants to go outside so will close now and walk with him to mail this letter.

Give our love to Leonard and the girls. Will write

again soon. You be sure to do the same.

Lots of love, Marion

St. Michael, Alaska
September 15, 1930

Dear Mother and Helen,
    I am going to write to both of you at once since I haven't time to write much before the *Vic* arrives.
    I have received several letters from both of you since I wrote last and thank you for all of them. I have been a little busy this summer and every time I started a letter something interrupted so I gave up trying. I have had to be on the job from six in the morning until anytime between six and midnight. It has been hard at times but lots of fun too. I did have a girl to wash dishes and make beds so that helped. And though I didn't get rich I did manage to make a few dollars for myself. The first month was the best and this month comes second. The most people I have fed at one meal is nineteen and that time I had only prepared for eight. It was funny when it was over but at the time I was hardly smiling. Then, too, I had days with almost no one coming in. I've been selling bread like a baker though, my largest order being for two dozen loaves. I had an awful time getting that much ahead since that was at the time of my biggest rush.
    This may be the last letter I shall write to you from St. Michael for some time. We have our government job; at least we were told to be ready to leave on short notice. We didn't get just the place we wanted but one a little farther away in the timber. It will seem funny to see trees again. The name of the place is Shaktoolik and it is about eighty miles from here. I am trying to pack, run

the restaurant and keep house at the same time. Needless to say, none of it is done any too well.

Today was a baking day. I baked two pies, a cake and six loaves of bread. Five of the loaves of bread were gone in half an hour so I will have to bake again tomorrow. I thought I would have a little time at home tomorrow but I guess that is not to be.

The *Ensee* left last Wednesday and won't be back until Thursday as the upper river boat is late. The *Vic* will get here about then too. I guess I won't see much of Kaurin until after his next trip.

When we leave here we will go to a place where we will be the only whites so we probably won't be on speaking terms by next spring. Anything to make a living!

Francis is having a few problems and doesn't look real well. We are hoping that the *Northland* comes here before we leave so that he can have his tonsils and adenoids out. I'm betting we'll have a nice (?) time on a boat with him. He was quite taken with them until the whistle scared him badly when we went to see someone off.

I wish I could visit all of you but am afraid that it will be a long time from now. We have had a miserable wet summer and I am tired and disgusted with the country. When we leave Alaska I want to go to a decent climate. But since I don't know where I want to go, I guess there's no use kicking up a fuss. There is not too much to worry one here so I suppose I am well off and just don't know it. I do hope times are picking up for you. They seem to be bad everywhere. They tell us that Seattle has had a bread line all summer, even one for women.

Brother Leonard is getting quite a family. How I'd love to see them all. Francis is wild about babies and I suppose should have a brother or sister but his mother has her hands full with him alone. Now he is always asking someone to play with him.

It is getting late. The fire is out and I am cold so will close and try and write again soon. I'll let you know our change of address as soon as we move.

Lots of love to both of you and moist kisses from Francis,

Marion

Chapter XII

Shaktoolik

The village of Shaktoolik is on the western fringe of the timber line and so, for the first time since arriving in Alaska, Marion is living among trees.

Her first school in Alaska was a public school for white and half-breed children. Now begins her first experience as a teacher of Eskimo children, under the direction of the Bureau of Indian Affairs. This was a challenging assignment inasmuch as she could not speak the language of the Eskimo and the children could not speak English.

Shaktoolik, Alaska
November 21, 1930

Dear Mother,
    We have actually moved. I left St. Michael the 30th
of September. It is only an eighty mile trip but it took
me two days to get here. Kaurin came two weeks later.
This place is really in the sticks but there is one other
white family here. I had met them before so they are not
complete strangers. They were the teachers here before
us but were fired for trading. They have two children,
one nine and the other Francis' age.
    Our first mail came two days ago. That's the only
communication we have with the outside. We have trees
here and are on a river, such as it is. Francis calls the
trees "dots of wood." The dogs were real excited with the
trees. They just ran all around them and kept looking up
at the tops. I almost felt like doing the same thing.
    I have been teaching since the 20th of October. It
was hard work getting started again after having been
away from it for so long. There are twenty-eight pupils
- the most I've had since leaving Chicago. We are getting
our Christmas program ready and as they are all in the
lower grades it is hard work.
    This job is through the Bureau of Indian Affairs and
all of my students are Eskimo. I have a difficult time
conversing with them. At first they just sat and listened
to me and would not say a word. I guess they are getting
used to me now though as they are beginning to talk a
little.
    Francis is learning to ski and he looks so funny! The
children in the school love to watch him and I have to
make him go where they can't see him out the windows
or I can't get them to do their work. Laughter seems to
have no language barrier.
    It is hard to realize that our little Francis is
beginning to grow up. He repeats everything he hears

and is a regular imp. He was terribly homesick for a month but he wasn't the only one.

Hope to hear from you soon.

Love from all, Marion

P. S. We have no P. O. here. Address us at
Shaktoolik, via Unalakleet, Alaska

Shaktoolik, Alaska
February 4, 1931

Dear Mother,

Had two letters from you this week. One went to St. Michael; also a card from Margaret and a letter from Jessie. You folks seem to visit around quite a bit. You don't know how I wish I could come and join you at it.

I manage to keep busy. I teach, have reindeer work to do as I am local reindeer superintendent, and also secretary and treasurer of the local reindeer company. I also do what medical work I can, which isn't much.

Kaurin does repair and carpenter work and such on the buildings and also teaches Trades and Manual Training to the boys and young men. Unless we are transferred to another school I will be here all summer as it is a year-around job. The school closes the first of May but I have more reindeer work in the summer and will have a kindergarten class for the summer. I don't care much for this place. I do miss my friends so much. We don't have much in common with the other white family here and that doesn't help. Also, the house here is very small; but we can stand it for a time. We are only a few feet from the river and the building will probably be moved in a year or two.

I scarcely get out of the house. We still have the three dogs that can sled but the days are too short to go out after school closes.   Saturdays I am too busy to get out and Sundays always seem to be stormy.

Francis is fine and just wants to live out of doors. We had a nice Christmas but rather lonely. Francis is still doing up packages and talking about Santa Claus and Christmas trees. He can't stop talking about the turkey we had on New Year's day, calls it a "Christmas boat" because we thawed it out in a tub of water.

This is a much colder place than St. Michael. On the 17th of November it was 33 below zero. Some cold for that time of year, believe me.

Well, I have reports to make out and more letters to write so must close for this time.

Lovingly, Marion

Shaktoolik, Alaska
February 18, 1931

Dear Helen,
Your nice letter of January 25 arrived an hour ago. The mail from the States goes through here to Nome on Wednesday and the mail from Nome goes through on Thursday. That gives us a chance to answer our letters at once if nothing interferes.

We are only about eighty miles north of St. Michael. It is much colder here and we have a colder house. Our potatoes are all frozen, a whole crate, so we will be out of them in a month. Then we will have to eat bread instead. It is a good thing we have canned stuff but there isn't a lot of that. Our eggs got too warm so they are not especially good either. I sure could use a good catering service about now.

We are about six miles from the coast by winter trail but more like sixteen (and it seemed sixty when I came up) by boat. We are right in the timber, such as it is.

Nothing like a forest in the states. Trees do not grow very large up here; too cold, I guess. The government is supposed to furnish our fuel but due to poor management last year, we are almost out so Kaurin went out and cut some trees down today. Francis was terribly excited over it and came to tell me that Daddy was knocking over the Christmas trees. You know there are no trees in or near St. Michael and I haven't seen a large tree since coming to Alaska. There are only black spruce, cottonwood and alders here. But we did have a pretty Christmas tree for the first time. We used an artificial one in St. Michael.

The job here really involves more social work than teaching. I teach, hand out medicines and anything else they want done. Kaurin is assistant teacher for only eight months so he can get away to go to St. Michael if he wants. I'm sure he will want to as he hates it here. He would like to start his boat and there are no tools here to do anything of that kind. Everything in that line is in St. Michael. We have asked for a transfer but do not know whether we will get it or not. It seems you just can't take a sailor away from the sea.

You asked about the subjects we teach here. They get the three Rs, of course and some practical and manual training. However, it makes hard going to teach sewing without thread or needles. I did find thirty yards of gingham. The whole setup is lacking items such as these. Poor Kaurin is in the same fix.

Not only is the teaching job difficult here but the household facilities leave us more than a bit frustrated. The river runs by the house and that is the water supply. And it is up to Kaurin to keep the lamps lit, carry the wood and ashes, and split the wood we use (which amounts to three cords a month and so no small job). What it all comes down to is - I'm lonesome way off here!

Kaurin hates it because I draw the largest salary but since he is free to work in the summer, he actually makes twice as much as I do. We did better last summer than we have for some time. I made a few dollars in the hotel and, believe me, I earned them. I liked doing it though, and so much better than this. The change is telling on me. I was as slender as you could wish but sure have put on the pounds out here. There is no place to walk and no place to go so I just sit around and "around" sure has spread. I have a cold continually too, something that did not bother me in St. Michael. About all the fresh air I get is going to school and back and it is about ten feet between the buildings. Are you getting the feeling that we aren't satisfied here?

I am beginning to long for a trip to the States so I am going to concentrate on that and maybe in the next hundred years or so we can manage it. I hope so.

We are in reindeer country but do not care much for the meat - and we have discovered that the bull that we bought for meat is too tough to eat. That means we must send to Nome for meat. The turkey was cheap, only fifty-five cents a pound but of course the postage is twelve cents a pound. Hopefully, we should be getting steaks, sausage and pork loin tomorrow. It seems sad that the arrival of meat should seem such a highlight in our lives.

Price changes do not affect us much up here. We got in our usual winter supply of food last fall. The other white family here has a trading post but not much stock. They scrimp much more on their food than we do. It seems as though there's so little else to spend money on, we feel entitled to all we want to eat.

This letter is rather long and I guess I haven't really said much, as usual. Give my love to all the family.

Lovingly, Marion

Chapter XIII

Baby Victor

By 1931, while the rest of the United States was in the throes of the depression, Marion and Kaurin began to emerge to a position of relative prosperity. Kaurin began to build his own boat and Marion finally got her coveted Delco electric plant.

Baby Victor was born on November 5, 1931, received the seal of approval from young Francis, and completed the Olsen family.

St. Michael, Alaska
September 10, 1931

Dear Mother,
     As you probably noticed by the return address, we are no longer at Shaktoolik. I am still working for the Bureau of Indian Affairs but have transferred to the village of Stebbins. It is a small place about twelve miles northwest of St. Michael - much more acceptable.
     Wish we were close enough to have you run up and see us once in a while. This would have been a nice summer for you as we had no mosquitoes for a change.
     I started school the first of September. I have just fourteen little Eskimo children this year. Francis goes with me since I have no one to leave him with. The girl that worked for me in the hotel is working elsewhere so I just take him along. I guess he does know an A when he sees it. And he talks plain enough - too plain sometimes.
     We had a warm summer and now will soon hole in for the winter. In six weeks or less we will be driving the dogs. We still have our three and should have two more but since it is hard to find any as fast as ours we will just forget about it.
     I don't suppose I will travel much this winter but Kaurin will go in at least once a week for the mail while he is out here. He won't stay here much though as he will be starting his boat this winter. The material came a couple of weeks ago. It will take a couple of years to finish it so we won't be using it next summer. He plans to build a skiff first, however, which we will use. There is a boat that belongs to this school which he uses now when he can get his engine to run. We expect a new six horse power on the next *Vic*. That's a big event for Kaurin.
     We finally have a portable electric light plant and, praise be, a washing machine. Kaurin is going to install

the light plant over here for me. Then if we want to move it to St. Michael in a year or so, we can. There are three there already. They don't cost much now.

I thought Shaktoolik was lonesome but this is almost as bad. I haven't seen a white person since the 12th of August except for Kaurin and Francis. There is only one Eskimo here who can speak or understand English, so I feel rather alone here. The school has been here for eight years but it only goes to the third grade.

This is a unique situation. The school furnishes toothbrushes and soda and the first thing we do each morning is brush our teeth. Then I pass out toilet tissue for handkerchiefs and doctor any sores they have. The first morning I handed out the tissue, Francis was all confused. He insisted I tell them the difference between the tissue and real handkerchiefs. Honestly, sometimes that child just knows too much for my good. In the first place, these Eskimos do not know what "toilet" means. And with that statement, I'm sure I don't have to tell you what a sanitation problem we have here.

The man has come for the mail so goodbye for now.

Love to all there,

Marion

St. Michael, Alaska
November 8, 1931

Dear Mother,
Just a note to let you know that the baby arrived O. K. and is a nice healthy boy. He was born November 5 and we have named him Victor Thornwald Olsen. We thought we wanted a girl but Victor is so good and he will make a good companion for Francis so we have decided to keep him.

Will write more later when I feel a little stronger.

Love, Marion

Stebbins, Alaska
February 8, 1932

Dear Mother,
Your letter of January 5 came a week ago so it made good time. Part of our mail service is by airplane but not very satisfactory. Sometimes the mail is quick and then another time it might be slower than by dog team.

The past three days have been one continuous blizzard with the last two days so bad that at times we haven't been able to see ten feet from the windows.

Kaurin did not get over to see us last week. He went to Kotlik. The store there burned down and he went over for the insurance company. I expected him to get back today but it has been too stormy. He will come over as soon as it clears enough to travel.

We are all well. The baby is the best ever and gets very little attention, it seems. The past four nights he has slept twelve hours straight. How I wish you could see him, Grandma.

I don't get out of the house much. I did go out for an hour yesterday, the first time since the 9th of January. There were some Eskimo twins born here that day and I went to see them; two boys. One had a tooth when he was ten days old but he only lived a couple of weeks.

These are busy days and I have a girl to help me now. I am teaching six days and two nights a week. In between times I am painting the living room. This is the first time I've ever wielded a paint brush and I think I've done a pretty good job. I have some more painting I want to do too but I am so busy. Every morning I build three fires, fix breakfast and dress the boys. By the time

I finish eating it is time for school, and after that the hours just fly by. There always seems so much to do.

My school has grown in the last two weeks. I have seventeen students now. Guess that will be all for this year and it is more than enough since they can hardly speak a word of English.

I don't know how many tons of coal I've used this winter but we use from 100 to 200 pounds a day. We started the season with 20 tons. It is Alaska coal and makes lots of ashes so we have to lug it in and then lug it almost all out again.

Well, the sun has finally come out so maybe we will see Kaurin in a couple of days.

Later in the day:

Kaurin came this afternoon. He got back to St. Michael yesterday. It sounds like it must have been a rough trip. He drove his own three dogs forty miles a day for two days, twelve miles the third day, forty miles a day for the next two days and then twelve miles over here. He had a load of about a hundred pounds besides the sled and himself all the time and we think our three dogs did themselves proud.

Feb. 10:

Kaurin went back to St. Michael today. It is 20 below zero and a strong wind blowing. I hated to see him leave and to see him leave in this weather made it even worse.

February 15:

This letter misses another mail. Kaurin did not come yesterday. We have been having an awful blizzard since Friday morning. It was so bad all the parents had to come for the children at noon. When they were ten feet away from the door they looked like shadows. So I've called it a day. It is 20 below zero now so it is impossible to keep the house warm.

February 17:
Kaurin came yesterday and went back this morning and I didn't send this letter along so will just continue it. Francis and I rode out to the lake when he left. I would so much like to take a trip to St. Michael myself when it gets a little warmer.

I guess all of you think I work harder than I do. Of course now that I have school six days and two nights a week, I am busy but I don't mind the work. It's much better than being idle. I have a few extra things such as one man who wants me to teach him how to knit socks and play the organ. I can handle the socks all right but I'm not much of an organist.

Well, by the time you wade through this you will be tired.

Lots of love, Marion

Stebbins, Alaska
March 23, 1932

Dear Mother,
This is probably the last time you will hear from me until navigation opens. They have cut off a number of our mail trips so the winter mail season is much shorter.

Francis has had the whooping cough, I guess. He did not really cough so much but was quite sick for awhile. I'm afraid I get rather panic stricken when the boys get sick. Actually Francis has been pretty healthy this year even though his tonsils are bad and need to be taken out. The simplest things can pose such a problem here.

I had visitors from St. Michael last Sunday. That's the first time any of them have been over to visit this winter.

It has been quite nice all month so I suppose April will be nasty. We have had a bad winter, cold and stormy with such awful blizzards.

Hard times have killed the reindeer business here and fur is worth nothing so the Eskimos are hard up. Most of them are living on meat and fish and the Red Cross flour won't come until next summer. Only one or two families at Stebbins are really destitute but most of the other villages are in bad shape.

The days are nice and long now. I don't have to light up until nearly seven. Seems good except that Francis objects to going to bed at seven now because it's still light.

One of the Eskimos just told me that I look sick. I told him that was one thing I have no time for. I want to have a garden this year. This house has a nice little cellar and if I can raise some turnips and carrots, I can keep them all winter. So you can picture me digging up the tundra soon. It all has to be done with a spade and I'm much too fat so it will be good for me.

Lovingly, Marion

Stebbins, Alaska
April 8, 1932

Dear Mother,
Me again. The days go by so fast with school, cooking, washing dishes and diapers, shovelling coal and ashes and sometimes snow that I've almost quit writing letters.

The days are nice and long now. It is light from about four in the morning until eight at night. But even that is not enough time to do everything. I let my girl go last month. She got quite lax and I figured if I had to do her work over again I might just as well do it the first time.

I have nineteen in school just now, not counting Francis.

April 14:

Since I started this I've been to St. Michael and the boss has been here by plane. He caused quite a sensation. The kids were out of the school house before I knew what was going on. This is only the second plane to land here.

April 21:

I don't believe I'll ever get this letter finished. School interferes too much with the things I'd like to do!

Kaurin came over yesterday morning and left in the evening. The snow is getting soft and it is poor travelling in the middle of the day. One of our dogs is lame so Kaurin only used two but still made good time. He had about fifty pounds besides himself on the sled. I plan to go over to St. Michael a week from today if the trail is good and I can get a team to take me. It will be Kaurin's birthday.

It seems funny to think that the farmers at home are starting their spring plowing and we are still snowed under up here. The banks around the house have gone down some but there is still much to go.

I have four weeks of school yet and after that I have the kitchen to paint, house to paint on the outside and my garden to plant. I'll have help with the top of the house since I'd be sure to fall off and break some bones.

April 23:

Kaurin is here again. Got here this morning before I was up. He left St. Michael about six and was here a quarter past seven.

Mail day has been changed again. There are only two more outgoing mails this spring so I can't delay this letter any longer.

Say, what is the news about the Lindbergh baby? Have they found the kidnappers yet?

Must close now and get to work. Give our love to all the family.

Marion

St. Michael, Alaska
July 14, 1932

Dear Mother,

I was glad to get your nice letter. It had been a long time since I heard from you.

It is raining, thank goodness. We needed it badly as we were almost out of water. There had been no rain for almost six weeks and my poor garden was almost dried up. Hope it does something now. We have had some radishes but the lettuce hasn't grown at all. The spinach, cabbage and turnips were doing the best. All my tomatoes died but I'm hoping to get a few potatoes. Disappointingly, the onions and some of the carrots never even came up. I suppose we will have an excellent crop of mosquitoes though when it stops raining and the sun comes out. We are all well and busy.

Wish I could join in some of the reunions you folks have and that you could come here once in a while.

I've been wanting Kaurin to go outside this fall and get his teeth fixed but I don't suppose he will. He says it would cost too much and has a few more excuses. I can't go for the winter and he can't go in the summer so there is no chance of our going together. I think that's the real reason he hates to go.

Francis is drawing pictures. He does quite well with a pencil and was very disgusted when I closed school. He thought he was quite a scholar.

The Evans have gone to the States to live and I'm now the only white woman in this part of the country. There is a nurse at Unalakleet, sixty miles away, and I guess it is a hundred or more in the other direction before you come to one. The school teacher's wife left him a year ago. Mrs. Hoelscher, the nurse, got sick and had to go to Seattle so I suppose there will be a new nurse at St. Michael soon. It would be nice to make a new acquaintance.

Must stop and feed the children. Write soon and tell me all the news. Love from all to all,

Marion

Stebbins, Alaska
December 14, 1932

Dear Mother,
Your last letter came a long time ago. I should have answered but it seems as though I'm always on the jump.

I was in St. Michael for a couple of weeks in August but as I had from four to six boarders three times a day, I wasn't exactly idle. I came back to Stebbins the 27th of August and from then on have been on the go constantly. We built a coalshed and after school started I painted the school room evenings. It seemed like an endless job but really is not a very big room.

I have twenty-two in school this year, ten of whom are beginners. Mr. Robinson, my boss, was here for two days just before Thanksgiving. He thought things were fine.

We are having lots of fun with our radio this winter. Last night we heard Chicago, Cleveland, Great Falls, Montana, Mexico, St. Louis, Salt Lake and of course all up and down the coast. We sometimes hear Hawaii, Australia and the Japanese. We have heard some of

Roosevelt's campaign speeches but have never picked up Hoover's.

It is strange to think of it being so cold in the States and to know that Chicago has a foot of snow. We haven't a speck. It was real cold for a couple of days two weeks ago and then it turned warm and melted our winter's supply of ice. It froze a little today but was warm enough so that Francis played out all day without mittens on. There is no going to St. Michael with the dogs unless they follow the sea and it is much farther that way, about twenty miles I guess. We had about two inches of snow but this warm spell took it all off.

Kaurin is here with me this winter. Just runs over to St. Michael for the mail some times. I went with him for Thanksgiving and hope to get over for Christmas. But if we don't get some snow I will have to walk. There are three white women there this winter. The teacher's wife came back, the commissioner got married after a twelve year engagement and a new nurse came in. She married the new wireless operator a couple of weeks after she arrived. Guess she didn't like living alone in the house. They say the poor man didn't stand a chance. She had heard about him on the boat coming up.

I am sending a little Christmas present from all of us. It will be late, I guess, as the airplanes can't fly around here just now.

Merry Christmas and happy new year.

Love from us,

Marion

Stebbins, Alaska
February 2, 1933

Dear Mother,

The card and your letter came during Christmas vacation. Thanks for both. Hope you got mine O. K.

We are having a terrible cold spell just now with a bad blizzard. The house is so cold, I can't seem to keep warm today. Just imagine, it is about 40 below zero. The cellar was down to 30 below, even with a lantern down there. Kaurin put down another and if that doesn't warm it up we'll have to put down the gasoline lamp and take the potatoes to bed with us. A lot of our potatoes froze when I was in St. Michael for Christmas.

We are all well. Had the flu just after New Year's and I had another attack of acute indigestion just after that. Then Kaurin and the boys had bad colds for ten days.

I have twenty-five students now but today is too cold for the small ones so only about ten came to school. This is only the second blizzard we've had this winter. The first one was two weeks ago. Kaurin was in St. Michael that time for four days. He got back in one day with only three dogs but the trail is bad now. We had only about an inch of snow up to the middle of January but have plenty now. Expect this month will be a fright. Have not been out of the house since New Year's day. I had our regular dinner party New Year's Eve, then came back to Stebbins the next day and haven't been out since. There are three women in St. Michael but they are all strangers to me so I don't care much about going over.

Victor has been walking for about two weeks and he thinks he's pretty smart. He is growing fast now, doesn't know many words yet though. He sees other people so seldom he is scared to death of them.

This winter has gone fast. We still have several months of it ahead of us but it seems as though it is almost over now that we don't have to get up in the dark to build fires.

Hope you are all well and that I'll be hearing from you soon.

Love to all,

Marion

Chapter XIV

A Visit Home

During the summer of 1933, Marion was able to leave Alaska for a trip to the States and a visit to the Chicago World's Fair. She took the two children on their first visit away from their Alaskan home, allowing them to meet their mother's family for the first time.

Stebbins, Alaska
April 29, 1933

Dear Helen,

Your letter came last week and I am outdoing myself in answering on the first outgoing mail.

By this time you will know that you will see the kids and myself in a few weeks, probably about the 10th of July. It may be a little later as I have to put in a few days at the Chicago Fair. I got my leave on that excuse. I can't tell you how anxious we are to see all of you again.

We haven't had any news for about a month now since we wore our radio batteries out. We have a new set now but reception is poor. There must be a lot to catch up on.

Today has been lovely so I stayed in and washed, made bread and so on. I hung clothes out for the first time this spring and it certainly improved their looks. They get so dingy from being dried in the house all winter.

I'm trying to get some clothes made for Victor. So far I have four night gowns and three rompers and should make about six more. They are plain as can be but so many button holes to make! I'm using plain color broadcloth and I love the colors. His wardrobe will look like a rainbow.

Just three more weeks of school. Then in May I must clean house; that means painting too.

If the ice does not go out early, we will have to walk to St. Michael. The Eskimos carry their babies on their backs so I'll hire one to carry Victor and I'll help Francis. It's about fifteen miles over rough tundra and through swamp. Can't you just see me? It will probably take about eight hours as I suppose Francis will have to rest often. I only hope we don't meet any bears. They are seen occasionally between here and there.

Will close for now. Six A. M. comes early.

Love, Marion

AFTER HER TRIP HOME

Seattle, Washington
August 29, 1933

Dear Helen,
    Your letter came today. If I had only known what
I know now I could have had another week with you.
The Alaska steamship *Aleutian* went on the rocks Sunday
so the *Vic* is making another trip to southeast Alaska and
won't leave here until the 12th for St. Michael. The
Victoria will take me to St. Michael. The *Ensee* is the
boat on which Kaurin works.
    If you want to write me a boat letter you address it
to me, c/o Alaska S.S. Company, Passenger on *S.S.*
Victoria sailing September 12 from Seattle, Washington.
    I took the kids for a street car ride this afternoon.
It's hard to know what to do with them in this small
apartment. Victor goes through all sorts of antics on the
street. He has an awful crush on the elevator boys here.
I don't know why it is unless it's their red uniforms.
They do look cute.
    The boys are in bed now but not asleep yet. The fire
engines have been screeching around here all evening.
They did last night too. Since there are a lot of big hotels
near here it makes me wonder if someone was smoking in
bed.
    Bye now. Will write again later.

Love, Marion

Stebbins, Alaska
December 3, 1933

Dear Helen,

Thank you for writing to Francis. He is so proud of his first letter.

We were seventeen days on the boat. I thought we would never get home. St. Michael was the ninth and last stop. Kaurin looked fine and gained nearly twenty pounds last summer. He's lost eight already. Do you suppose that's indicative of anything? I don't think I'll try to find out.

This is the first year since I've been in St. Michael that someone hasn't had a Thanksgiving party. I couldn't give one because the house was so upset (we are remodeling), so I just stayed at Stebbins. I came here the 5th of October and have been here ever since. Mrs. Hillman, the nurse from St. Michael, has been made travelling nurse and should be here soon to stay for a while. That will be nice for me.

It is ten above zero today. Not much like last summer. I have nineteen in school now and don't know if the rest are coming or not. There should be six more to come. It's already time to start preparing for our Christmas program. It doesn't seem as though Christmas is so near because we missed our Thanksgiving party.

I know this is terribly short but just wanted you to know that we are thinking of you.

Love, Marion

Stebbins, Alaska
January 23, 1934

Dear Mother,

Your letter came last week and I'm going to answer

now before I put it off for six months.

We have been having awfully cold weather since the first of the year. It has been almost fifty below here and St. Michael has been worse. It was down to sixty below over there. That is awfully cold here on the coast. It warmed up the other day and snowed but is colder again today.

I have twenty-eight in school now when they are all here. Most of the time there are about twenty-four and they sure keep me busy. I used to be able to write letters in school but not with this bunch.

There have been two deaths and four births since school started. There was a set of twin girls born a few weeks back. They are as small as dolls but so homely, poor little things. One of my oldest school girls is very sick. I think she has T.B.

The nurse was here two days last week. There was no one sick then, of course. I don't think travelling nurses will prove very satisfactory. They never seem to be around when needed.

My boys are more noisy now that they are shut in. The place is so small here they seem to be under foot all the time.

I am knitting socks and mittens for my family. That could keep me busy all the time. We could buy them, of course, but the handmade ones are so much warmer.

We went to St. Michael for Christmas. Stayed a couple of days, came back here for a couple more and then went to St. Micks again for New Year's Eve. I gave my usual New Year's Eve dinner and came back here the first. Of course my boss had to show up and catch me off the job. He said he thought it was time for our celebration and that he would get in on a good dinner. He did, too. I had grapefruit/grape juice cocktail, roast turkey, dressing, corn, string beans, baked hubbard squash, lime salad, hot rolls, mashed potatoes, hot apple pie, coconut cake, and of course coffee, nuts, candy, pickles, olives, spiced figs, cranberries and jelly.   I thought I did well in such a short time, don't you? One of my neighbors helped me serve but I did the rest myself.

The radio reception is coming in good and clear tonight. Last night we listened to the Flagship America. It came through K. S. L. at Salt Lake City. We get London quite often in the morning between eight and ten.

Give my best to all of the family and I'll write them soon.

Love from all of us,

Marion

Stebbins, Alaska
February 25, 1934

Dear Helen,
I've taken pity on Kaurin and I think he's gained back that eight pounds. At least he's not thin. Now you can stop worrying - or maybe it's me that can stop.

Santa was good to me. I got an electric mixer, an apron, lace table cloth, luncheon set, tray, casserole, and two pairs of silk stockings. The children and Kaurin did equally well.

We had a very happy wedding anniversary too. Some of my friends gave me some beautiful linens.

The wolf was at our door yesterday. I don't mean the poverty wolf - we literally had a wolf at our door. Our dogs barked while I was putting lunch on the table and I looked out to see what the disturbance was. There, about seventy-five feet from the house, was an animal that I took to be a fox. I called Kaurin to come and see and he said its legs were too long for a fox, that it must be a wolf. Sure enough, a few minutes later an Eskimo came along with a dog team and they were chasing the

thing. Several teams turned out to join the chase but the
teams finally had to give up. A man who was on foot
finally got it. It must have been hungry to come so near
a settlement. I have never known them to come so near
the coast.

On Washington's birthday we went out with the dogs
and took some movies. They should be good as our dogs
go crazy when anyone is in front of them and they just
tear. Kaurin went ahead and took pictures of me driving
up to him, then I took some of him.

It is bed time so I must close. Only ten or twelve
more weeks of school. How time flies.

Love to all,

Marion

Chapter XV

Summer School and the Burning of Nome

Like all good school teachers, Marion felt she had to keep up on the latest teaching techniques. As a means of doing this, she attended school at Nome during the summer of 1934. It was a difficult time because she was alone with the two children. However, it was a pleasing diversion from her usual routine as she made new acquaintances and enjoyed the fellowship of old friends and fellow teachers.

A few weeks after Marion left Nome, the wooden city was nearly destroyed by fire. Carpenters and lumber soon arrived, however, and a new Nome made its appearance from the ashes.

Stebbins, Alaska
September 9, 1934

Dear Mother,

Sorry I haven't been writing but I am back on the job now and will try to catch up. My vacation is over and school opened last week with seventeen students. There should be more before long.

I left Nome the 11th of August and took the boat that Kaurin owned when I met him. It is now on the run between Nome and St. Mike. We left Nome about 8:00 o'clock Saturday night and were in St. Michael Monday afternoon at 2:00. We had a good trip except for a few hours Sunday night, just long enough to make me seasick. Thankfully, the boys didn't get sick. The boat was crowded and there is no place for passengers to sit now that she has been rebuilt; so I stuck Victor in the berth as soon as we got on board. He began to entertain everyone by playing seasick at once. We came over to Stebbins on the barge from St. Michael and he really did get seasick then. The trip took five hours and was quite rough.

I had a good time in Nome but it cost quite a bit. I had to have someone to care for the boys while I went to school and that cost me exactly $250 for the six weeks. My fare and room rent were paid for by the government. It was fun to have people to talk to. I met a lot of them last fall on the *Vic* and of course I knew quite a few Nome people. There were thirty-five teachers there. They had banquets, dances and parties as well as school work. It was a nice interlude.

I spent two weeks in St. Michael on my way home so had a nice visit with Kaurin. He was working in the shipyard and staying at home. He left the day before I did.

We have had a cold, stormy summer and my poor garden didn't do anything this year. Of course the radishes went to seed before I got back. The lettuce is small and bitter and we only had one meal out of the potatoes and one out of the turnips.

We have all been well for most of the summer except for a couple of days that I was sick while in Nome. The Eskimo kids scared Francis so badly he was almost sick. They are all afraid of the dark and have been telling him all kinds of things. I have been trying to get him over it but curing him is harder than scaring him.

Tomorrow is another school day so I guess I'd better close for now. I'm always sleepy in the morning.

Lovingly, Marion

Stebbins, Alaska
October 6, 1934

Dear Mother,

Your letter came a long time ago and I meant to answer much sooner. Time seems to slip by so fast when school is in session.

I started school the day after Labor Day and also started supervising a gang of men the same day. There are no white men in Stebbins right now so I have to act as foreman as well as teacher. I've had from three to six men working since we started. It makes a lot of extra reports and I got so far behind I had to take a day from school yesterday to catch up. That, with housework and janitor work, has kept me busy. I have time to write at night but lack ambition after the kids are in bed. I must pick up some ambition somewhere as I have a lot of sewing and knitting to do.

We have a new radio that is a dandy. You can't begin to imagine how quickly we wear them out because we play them so much. Anyway, our new one is a ten-tube and I am really enjoying it. It came a week ago.

All of my winter supplies came then too and the captain of the boat that brought them over set up my radio for me. It is a cabinet and as pretty as can be with a much fuller tone than my old one. It is an all-wave and I've had Australia, France and Germany.

We have four dogs this year. One was given to us this summer. He is only a year old so is not broken to work as yet but we hope to make a leader of him. His name is Palooka. It's about two syllables too long for a team dog. I wanted to change it to Bill but Francis wouldn't stand for it. He claims him as his own since this dog is smaller and more of a pet than the old dogs.

We left our dogs with an Eskimo while we were gone to Nome and when we came back they were nearly starved. I think our best dog would have been dead in two more days. I don't believe they had been watered in days. Beans was too weak to chew dry fish and couldn't stand on his feet. I babied him along on mush for nearly a week before he could chew the fish. The worst thing was that they acted as though they had been beaten. Now when they see me they wag all over.

I haven't seen Kaurin for almost a month and I don't expect him for another ten days. I do wish he could come over more often as it is lonesome here, the evenings especially.

I had a good time in Nome but about two weeks ago Nome burned down almost entirely. The fire started in an old three-story hotel. I suppose there was a high wind and the fire protection wasn't adequate. The whole business district burned; all the stores, the bank, post office, court house, jail and the coast guard buildings. The club house burned too and a lot of homes. Two ships of lumber and supplies were rushed up from Seattle and any one who can do carpenter work can have a job. The Polet's store burned down several years ago and he had just gotten it all built up again and a lovely home and green house. Now it's all gone again. They dynamited their home trying to stop the fire. Even the fire station burned.

Francis said he was glad the dentist's office burned down since he doesn't want his teeth filled again. He had seven done this summer.

September was quite nice here and today we have our first snow. It was just a year ago yesterday that I got back here from my trip to the States.

Jessie wrote that your summer was too hot for her. I don't believe I could have stood it. I ran around Nome this summer in those pink and white wash silk dresses and a calico jacket and half of the women were wearing fur coats with collars turned up over their ears. The boys have been wearing their summer underwear until today. I put them into woolens this morning. Francis said it felt good. I wear rayon.

Must close. Write soon.

Love to all,

                                        Marion

Stebbins, Alaska
December 19, 1934

Dear Helen,

It's been a long time since your letter came but as I had already written about the fire there wasn't much to write about. No lives were lost although there were a few burns, of course. Those two Eskimos that were missing had only gotten drunk and gone to sleep somewhere. You heard about the fire before I did. It was before we got our new radio and the old one was not working.

Kaurin has been appointed U. S. Commissioner for St. Michael. I don't know as he will take it. It is a lot of grief and he would have to keep his other job since the commissioner's job does not pay a salary. I am not doing any encouraging, believe me. We have managed to keep out of scrapes so far but I'm afraid we'd be too involved with that business.

Christmas is creeping up on me. We will go to St. Mike as usual. Francis was writing to Santa tonight and wrote each of his requests on a separate sheet so Santa wouldn't get them mixed. He asked for skates; all the boys here have them. That is the only thing he asked for that I don't have. But skating will soon be over for the heavy snow is about due. The trail to St. Mike is terribly rough right now because the snow is so scarce as yet.

Our old dogs don't show their age any when it comes to speed. Kaurin made a round trip to the city yesterday. He didn't leave until about eleven and was back by half past four, even resting in St. Michael for a few hours. The old sled is like the old one-horse shay; it's all going to fall apart some day soon. Kaurin wires it up with bailing wire every time he uses it but slow dogs would be better for it on this kind of trail. A new one would cost fifty dollars or more.

I am finishing my Christmas knitting and getting ready to leave for St. Michael on Sunday. We will have the school party on Friday but I'm afraid it won't be too much. It's rather difficult to prepare a program when there isn't much of the audience that will be able to understand English.

Merry Christmas and lots of love to all,

Marion

Chapter XVI

<u>Lonely Days at Stebbins</u>

In 1935 Marion was occupied with the Bureau of Indian Affairs at Stebbins and Kaurin was busy at St. Michael and working on his boat there. The long days, mosquitoes and loneliness begin to overwhelm Marion and for the first time we hear of her desire to leave Alaska for a permanent home in the States.

Stebbins, Alaska
January 3, 1935

Dear Helen,

The patterns and your letter arrived just before Christmas. Thanks for both. The pattern was very easy but my material wasn't very good. I only paid fifteen cents a yard for it so I guess I couldn't expect much. My Eskimo friends admire it anyway.

We have been having mild weather again with only about a week of real cold weather so far. We went to St. Michael for Christmas, as usual, but did not wait for New Year's. We were afraid our foodstuff would freeze in the cellar here. Kaurin came over once and filled the lanterns. I had my celebration dinner on the Friday before New Year's but it was sort of a fizzle. There are only five people left there to invite. But we had a good time, just us few.

Our turkey was late coming and we had to eat ham instead. I suppose we will go over in a month or so and eat the turkey.

The boys have been out all day today sliding down the hill. Francis has a sled but Victor uses an old tin wash basin. They really had a good time. It is such a relief when they can stay out of doors. With two active boys around the house seems even smaller than it is.

Lots of love,

Marion

Stebbins, Alaska
April 14, 1935

Dear Mother,

This is probably the last chance I will have to get a letter out to you on the winter mail. The ice is gone in so many places that the trails will soon disappear.

Kaurin starts work tomorrow, two weeks earlier than usual. He left here for St. Michael today. This will be a long summer for me as he will be gone more than usual. The *Ensee* will run up to Holy Cross this year on all her trips. That means no layovers in St. Mike like they have had other years.

We are all well now. Kaurin and the boys had the flu and Kaurin is not quite over his cold. He needs his teeth fixed so badly. I think he ought to go out next winter but I don't want to quit my job then unless I have to and he doesn't want to go without the family.

March was a terrible month. It stormed all the time. So much snow piled up around the house that the natives had to shovel it away from the door before we could get out. Both doors are on the same side of the house and they were both snowed under. We have even more snow than four years ago.

I have been busy knitting, as usual. It is a perpetual job with so many men in the family. All the socks seem to give out at once. Thank goodness one pair of legs are good for a couple of feet!

How I wish I could borrow an electric iron for a few hours. I have a huge ironing to do. That is the one thing I can never seem to get done. I don't get up early enough in the morning and I'm too tired to tackle it after school. Well, tomorrow I'll have to do it or it will rot away.

School will close in about two weeks and I will be glad to finish. I would like to get away for a while after school is out but that just won't be possible. The trail will be gone by that time and there is no place to go. I have not been to St. Michael since Christmas and have seen only one white woman since then and one white man outside of my own family. But as I am pretty sure this next year will be our last in Alaska, I guess I will survive.

We have nice long days now. It doesn't get dark

until eight o'clock. I'll miss the daylight summers if we ever do go to the States to live.

Must close. Write again soon. Love to all,

Marion

Stebbins, Alaska
June 9, 1935

Dear Mother,

Summer has finally arrived, I guess. We had such a late, cold spring that I was beginning to think it would never get warm. The ice is all gone from in front of our place and I guess it is all gone at St. Michael now too. Kaurin was over here last week but it is too far to walk very often. The boys and I walked part way over and back one day. I did not know just how far it was from where we were so did not dare go on. We were all pretty tired when we got back home.

We have been watching for a boat to go by here but haven't seen any as yet. That would mean summer was here for sure.

I have been knitting mittens out of odds and ends so they are all colors of the rainbow. The boys admire them a lot. I have taught Francis to do plain knitting. He can cast on stitches and has a piece that he started last winter that he says is to be a wristlet. Of course he drops stitches sometimes and pulls his yarn too tight but he will get over that in time if he continues knitting.

I have just finished painting the school room and our bedroom. The bedroom was small and easy but that schoolroom seemed endless. It is only 24 x 18 but the ceiling seemed as big as a forty acre farm while I was painting it. Well, it is the last time I expect to do it. Someone else can do it next time. I suppose it is foolish to plan so far ahead. Our plans always seem to go wrong when we do.

The boys are home and say they are hungry. That is about the only time I see them. They are well and on the go every minute they are out of bed. They have good appetites too. I am out of potatoes and give them mush two and three times a day. I cook it in the morning, fry what is left over for lunch and they have dry cereal for supper. They don't seem to mind it at all.

I haven't much of a kitchen garden so far. I do have some sweet peas and nasturtiums in the house and some pansies out of doors. I also started some swiss chard and some lettuce in the house but it froze after I planted it out of doors.

We received all the Easter cards, thanks. The boys were very proud of theirs and Victor carried his until he wore it out. Everyone he saw had to look at it. The cards came the week after Easter so you timed them pretty well.

Lots of love from all of us,

Marion

Stebbins, Alaska
June 25, 1935

Dear Mother,

Your letter of May 5 came on the first boat. I went over to St. Michael for a few days and was there when the boat arrived.

I will be here in Stebbins all summer, I guess, as I did not ask for a leave this year. There is no one in St. Michael and no one here. Kaurin was so busy while I was over there that he was not home at all. He won't be so busy from now on so I suppose I will go over soon again if there is anyone here to feed the dogs for me. We still have four of them. Kaurin wanted me to have one of them killed but I can't bear to have it done. The poor old dog is getting too slow and does not do much to help in the team. It costs about a dollar a month to feed a dog.

A boat load of Eskimos is just pulling out, leaving here for the summer. There are only a couple of families left now.

Talk about hot! It is eighty in the shade. That isn't hot for you but it is terribly hot here. I think every day that it will rain but it hasn't as yet and the garden needs rain badly. Some things are turning yellow already. I have been watering it but that does not seem to do much good. We will have radishes to eat in a few days. Some of the pansies are in bloom already. They came along fine after I planted them outside. I kept the nasturtiums in the house and they are budded too. The willows leafed out overnight after it turned warm. It was so cold in May and the first of June that I didn't think it would be worthwhile to try gardening at all but it is farther along than usual.

I have been fixing over some old dresses but won't make any new ones until I get some goods and patterns. We did not get a summer Sears catalog this year so guess I will have to ask someone to pick out some goods and send it to me. I am wearing old ragged house dresses now to save my new ones for school this fall. I have one on now that I put in the rag bag five years ago and for some reason the rag was never used so this spring I fished it out and used it while I was painting. It isn't ragged, just faded and I guess that was why I threw it away. The kids look as though I had pulled them out of the rag bag too. They are wearing out all their old things so as to have decent clothes when school starts. The material for their suits isn't here yet but should be on the next boat. That should keep me busy for awhile.

Kaurin is still up-river. They went up a week ago. Of course I may have missed seeing them as they pass a couple of miles from here and might have gone by in the night.

We are all well but bitten up with mosquitoes. They are out in full force. Before we went to St. Michael, Victor's eyes were swollen shut from their bites. They can be quite vicious.

Must stop and get busy. Love from the whole tribe,

Marion

Stebbins, Alaska
July 1, 1935

Dear Helen,

Well, winter is beginning again, as one of our Eskimo friends always says. At least we are past the longest day. It seems to me that it is darker at night already.

I was pleased to get your nice long letter. The samples of your dresses are very pretty. I wish I could buy a couple of ready-made ones for myself.

The weather is warm and no rain yet. The yard is full of bluebells and they are very fragrant and pretty. I hope there will be some berries this year. Francis brought in some cranberry blossoms the other day.

I am not taking a vacation this year. I am saving it so I can take it just before I resign. I don't know yet just how I am going to work things. It would be nice for Kaurin if I could get away from here about the first of May but that is too close to the closing of school and I will have to clean the place up for the incoming teacher.

The valley you mentioned where they are sending the farmers is far from us. It is about a hundred miles from Anchorage, four days run on a steamer direct from Seattle. It is a big thing for Anchorage, but Alaska is having to ship destitute people out of the country and the government did not give any work to Alaskans at all. They shipped in a lot of people to clear the farms and put up houses. It is a questionable project at best. I suppose these farmers call themselves pioneers but the government appears to be doing everything for them. I'll bet a lot of them were ready to leave after they met the mosquitoes. There was a woman in St. Michael that had just come from that part of the country and she said they were wading around ankle deep in mud there. That may be better farming country than this but we aren't and haven't been wading in mud. That is one nice thing about Stebbins. It is on a sand bar and is always dry.

The *Ensee* is in St. Michael. They went by yesterday. I have been looking for them to come by again today as they are due at Marshall in a few days again. Can you imagine keeping track of your husband by watching his boat go by? Going home to the States looks better to me all the time.

St. Michael is just as lonesome as this place this summer. Mrs. Johnston went out for the summer so there is not a white woman anywhere near here. So for my sake, please write often.

The boys are well but badly bitten up with mosquitoes. I have a few bites but am not out of doors much.

The dish water sounds hot so will go make use of it before it all boils away.

Love, Marion

Chapter XVII

End of a Career

The school year of 1935-1936 was the last year Marion was to teach. Her plans for leaving Alaska were now well formulated. She busied herself cleaning, painting, equipping and improving so as to leave her school and her work in better condition than when she arrived.

Stebbins, Alaska
August 23, 1935

Dear Mother,

I am in hopes that Kaurin will be over in a few days and take this to St. Michael to mail. He is up river now but should be back tomorrow or the next day. Poor dear, he is suffering so with his teeth. I do want him to go to Seattle this fall and get them fixed.

The boys and I were out picking berries all day today. They are rather scarce; we pick one and have to walk a mile to find another. We did get a couple of gallons. We have to stay where we can see the bay as the *North Star* should have been to St. Michael now and our freight will be coming any day.

I put up nine pints of salmon berries and ten of cranberries but will be getting short of sugar. That strike on the coast is holding up the loading of the boats so they are all awfully late getting here. The one that was to leave the 12th of this month has not left yet and some of my stuff should be on it.

Right now, with fresh berries and garden stuff, we are living high. If the ptarmigan were only large enough to eat it would be fine. My lettuce headed up nicely and we are eating all the head lettuce we can stuff down now. The turnips are large enough to use too. The potatoes have the largest tops I have ever seen on them up here so maybe they are all tops.

I have a kettleful of orange marmalade on the stove and how I hate the smell! I am trying to get everything done before time to start school. I get rushed at this time of year but somehow things always manage to get done.

The Eskimos are all berrying. This afternoon when we came home through the village, every house had a padlock on it. There isn't one person in the village. I can't tell you what an eerie feeling it gave me. It makes me realize how unbearably lonesome my life would be without the boys.

It is Saturday morning and the *Ensee* is anchored out in front. Guess it is too rough for them to go around the point as they are towing a barge. It rained a little in the night so we won't go berrying today. I guess I don't really need an excuse to stay home though. I don't expect Kaurin will get ashore as they are pretty far out.

Breakfast is ready so must go and get the boys in the house. They had to go watch the boat.

Love, Marion

Stebbins, Alaska
September 3, 1935

Dear Helen,

Your letter came today and although I won't be able to mail this for some time I am going to answer it before I forget what I want to say.

The government freight came today and since the boat left I have been opening crates and boxes and checking. I had ordered quite a bit of stuff for the school and I feel tonight as though my back had been broken.

Thanks for going to all that trouble of getting the material for me. I certainly ought to be the best dressed woman in Stebbins. A few weeks after I wrote you I got hold of a catalog and ordered some material for myself. All cotton. I had to smile about your saying I could wear silk in the school room. I wear nothing but calico as a rule so that if I spill a quart of cod liver oil or some such thing on myself I will not feel very badly about having to throw the dress away. I once spilled a whole ounce of that red antiseptic on a dress that I was wearing for the first time. I did manage to wash that out but some things won't come out. Anyway, I appreciate your getting the material for me and maybe I can help you out some time (how I'd love the chance).

Speaking of dresses, I had some old rayon net curtains, years old. They were rose and silver trimmed with a heavy rose fringe. The other day I gave them to one of the Eskimo girls. I asked her if she knew what they were and she said she did. Imagine my surprise this morning to see Winnie decked out in a dress made of those curtains and trimmed all around the hem with the fringe. Underneath she had a plaid gingham shirt and a pair of green silk pants that I had given her. I could scarcely keep my face straight. I finally decided that the only thing I could do was to give her an old dress of mine and tell her to keep the rose one for parties. If you live in one place long enough up here you're apt to meet not only yourself but your furnishings coming and going.

I heard the other night that twenty-three farmers (mostly from Michigan) had left Matanuska. They said it was a case of too many bosses. I expect they have plenty of them all right. The few people I have met are of divided opinions about that project. Alaska's biggest criticism is that there was no employment given to Alaskans. There is no question that they can raise crops but where in the dickens are they going to sell them? There seems to be some problem about selling the stuff right here in Alaska. We haven't been too informed about the project here.

I am going to quit now and have a cup of tea.

Love, Marion

Stebbins, Alaska
September 8, 1935

Dear Mother,

The *Ensee* should be going by today so I hope to send this over to the post office before it is a month old. I would like to go over to St. Michael myself. I started school last week but I really think the few children that are here should be picking berries for the winter anyway.

We have had more than our fill of berries. Victor even refused to eat blueberries for breakfast this morning. He turns down lettuce now too. We have eaten lettuce once and sometimes twice a day for over a month now and it's just too much for him. Francis and I still enjoy it though. I have given much of it away but still have a lot.

You don't seem to have much more company than I have but I guess you do see more people. The only white people that I have seen since the fourth of August were here on the *Meteor* the other day with the freight. They were the captain of the boat, Frank Williams the owner and the U.S. Marshall at St. Michael. They were all so busy though that I didn't talk to them much. They were only here two hours and as they had over twenty tons of stuff to unload, they didn't have much time to visit.

We will be pretty busy here this fall as I have a lot of stuff to repair the building with. We are going to line it with new insulating board all through and that will mean all new doors, window frames and baseboards. Also will have my painting to do over again. I have two new stoves, a heater for the school room and a range. I haven't unpacked the range yet but know it is black. Ranges burn out so fast here because we force them so. The old range is all humps and hollows. It will seem good to be able to push a pan around on top of the stove and not have it hit a hump and upset.

There is an authorization of $350 for this station, including coal. I must have exceeded it by $150 or more this year but they sent everything that I ordered. Part of the stuff is not here yet but it has been shipped. It is still on the *North Star*, I expect.

We are all quite lonesome here. Victor just asked if we could go to St. Michael and stay for a long time.

Must close. Write soon.

Love to all, Marion

Stebbins, Alaska
September 22, 1935

Dear Helen,

I was over in St. Michael a week ago and the goods for the dresses arrived. They are all lovely. Thank you so much. I believe I will wait a while to make these up as I am so thin right now. If I made them to fit now I am sure they would be too small by spring. I am down to 107 now but am sure to gain when Kaurin is home.

The *Ensee* came by here on the 12th and Kaurin came ashore to see us. I had supplies in St. Mike and knew that I could get back by boat so I took the boys and went over with him. We got there late in the afternoon and stayed on the boat for supper. After eating, Kaurin and Capt. Hoelscher went over onto the barge to look at some freight. When they started to climb back aboard the *Ensee* Kaurin's foot slipped and he landed with his full weight on his chest on the railing which is only an iron pipe. It knocked him out and after he came around enough we went to shore. We could feel one broken rib but could not be sure of the other. The teacher came and we strapped him up as best we could. He went back to work the next day but felt pretty punk, I guess. I haven't seen him since. Capt. Hoelscher said he was to have a man with him in the pilot house but of course he couldn't do any lifting of freight. Kaurin was going to see the doctor at Mt. Village on the way up-river. It came at a bad time as he must finish out the year in order to qualify for the large bonus when the season ends.

Francis spent the day building a doghouse for

Palooka and then, after all his work, the cur wouldn't go into it. I saw Francis and Victor pushing and lifting but the pup refused to go inside. They are learning the definition of frustration.

I have been busy readying my plants for winter. It has been snowing the past two or three days so I dug up my Pansies and put them in a window box. Also transplanted some other plants. It really isn't cold today but there have been several snow flurries.

The dogs are telling me it is supper time. We feed them at 5:00 o'clock and they are beginning to register complaints as it is twenty minutes after.

Love from all of us,

Marion

Stebbins, Alaska
November 28, 1935

Dear Mother,

I don't believe I have written to you for three months. The past month has been a busy one. Kaurin came over on the 25th of October and on the following Monday started the carpenter work on the building. The whole place is now insulated by wall board one-half inch thick. Some of the window and door casings are not finished but we will just keep plugging away until it is all done. All the reaching has evidently pulled Kaurin's broken rib apart where it was healing and he is having to let it heal again. Other than that, we are all well.

Radio reception has been poor all fall until about a week ago. There is a little static tonight but not much. We are able to hear all the news again.

If the weather is good we are going to St. Michael tomorrow for Thanksgiving dinner. The white population has grown. There will be fifteen at the party, six of them children under eleven. It should be noisy if not fun! I haven't seen any of the newcomers yet. I was over last Saturday for a couple of hours but the weather was so bad and my time so short that I made no calls.

I have been making sail cloth parkas for the boys. They have no fur ones this year and the cotton ones break the wind and make their snowsuits about warm enough. I haven't done any of my own sewing yet. You know how it is, Mama's things always come last. I have much I could go on and do tonight but I am so tired. I made bread today and a dishpan of crackerjacks for the school children.

Kaurin, the boys and I join in wishing you a Merry Christmas and Happy New Year.

Lots of love,

Marion

Stebbins, Alaska
February 9, 1936

Dear Mother,

Your letter and Helen's came last week. Thanks very much for them.

The weather still stays nice. It is cold but clear and we can notice that the days are lengthening. We don't light up until 4:00 o'clock now.

We are all well, as usual. The boys do a lot of talking about going to Seattle next fall. Francis said once that he didn't want to go until after Christmas for fear Santa Claus wouldn't be able to find him. They were talking about the pets they want. Francis wants a cat but Victor was more original. He informs me that he would like an owl and a pig.

I didn't tell you what Santa brought me this last

Christmas.   He evidently expects me to travel as he
brought a steamer wardrobe trunk.   Also a carpet
sweeper, one of the streamlined ones and two pretty silk
slips. We all had a lovely holiday.

We had beans and Boston brown bread for supper
tonight and they have made me thirsty. That doesn't
sound like much of a Sunday dinner, does it? We are out
of fresh meat just now but have some coming from Nome
soon. We have lots of ham, bacon and canned meat
though. Francis has snares set for ptarmigan but has not
caught any as yet.

Must quit and get started at my reports. Francis is
requesting help with his valentines too.

Lovingly, Marion

Stebbins, Alaska
March 29, 1936

Dear Mother,
The birthday card came last week. It was so pretty.
Thanks much. The boys were quite envious. We had a
cake on your birthday so didn't have one on mine. We
had my favorite pie instead.

We have had two days of spring-like weather for a
change. The snow went down a great deal and it is warm
enough so that we don't have too much fire. I did not do
my ironing today because it was so warm and the boys
were in the house all day. Francis had a touch of snow
blindness and Victor's eyes were red so we kept them in
to recover. I kept ice on Francis' eyes for a couple of
hours. That seemed to do more good than anything.
There is so much snow and it is so white. The glare is
terrible when the sun shines. The boys have been staying
out of doors from 8:00 in the morning until 5:00 or 5:30
in the afternoon and have gotten quite tanned.

Yesterday, while I was down in the village, some of the boys were running around barefoot in the snow and today we saw a bunch of them on the roof of a house sitting in the sun without a stitch of clothes on. Someone wrote a parody on "When it's Springtime in the Rockies" and called it "When it's Springtime in Alaska." There is one line in it that goes, "And the Eskimos go barefoot in twenty feet of snow." That isn't as ridiculous as it sounds.

Only five more weeks of school and I am through teaching for good. I can hardly believe it myself. I plan to stay here for a couple of months after school is out since I won't be able to get away until the boats start running and the first rush of spring work is over.

Three weeks ago the daughter of the school teacher in St. Michael died of diabetes. She was only sick for about a week but they know now that they just did not recognize the symptoms. She died in the plane while they were taking her to the hospital. It is so sad but it makes me even more certain that we are doing the right thing by getting our children closer to good medical care.

The radio has been almost useless this winter. We just can't seem to get anything in the evening.

Love from all,

Marion

Chapter XVIII

Farewell to Alaska

Farewells are always sad and there was to be no exception for Marion and her family. It was hard to say goodbye to the settlers that she had come to know so well over the years but even more difficult to bid farewell to the Eskimos who had come to depend on this little school teacher, nurse and friend.

St. Michael, Alaska
June 14, 1936

Dear Mother,

Well, I am no longer a working woman. I left Stebbins for good on the 7th of June. The summer arrived early so I was able to get away sooner than I had expected. However, I will be drawing my pay until the last of August as I have three months leave and my salary must not overlap the new teacher's whose salary will start the first of September.

The Eskimos did not want me to leave. I think they believe I have been fired as they have written a petition to Juneau to get me back. I guess they just can't conceive of anyone quitting a job of his own will. It won't do anybody any good but it won't do me any harm either. I must admit to tears at their declarations of love. When the boat came to get me they all came to see me off and helped me to get ready. They had been saying all spring that they didn't want me to leave. I thought they were just trying to make me feel good but I guess they really meant it.

We had a lovely day to come over. I had a feeling all last week that there would be a boat on Sunday and so hurried up the house cleaning. Had just shellacked the floors Saturday so the place will look fair when the new teacher gets there. Now I have plenty of cleaning to do here.

Just three weeks before we left Stebbins the boys and I walked over here to St. Michael. Francis didn't get tired but Victor gave out and I had to carry him most of the time for about five miles. Then he decided to walk and finished the last three miles on his own feet. It turned cold and rained for a while and it wasn't so very nice walking. We started from Stebbins at 7:00 in the morning and got to St. Michael at 1:00 p.m. Kaurin was really surprised. Some of the Stebbins children were here and saw us coming and began to yell. I couldn't have gone much farther. I had gotten to the place where if I stopped walking to wait for Victor, I could hardly start again. Kaurin got one of the boys to take us back with a dog team. It took almost as long to get back as dogs don't go very fast over bare ground. However, I must admit it beats walking!

The mosquitoes have been out for several weeks now. They were in the house yesterday and I was fighting them all night. Poor Victor is all bitten up.

In about three months I will be on my way to Seattle if all goes well. It still doesn't seem real. The boys are making all sorts of plans but Kaurin and I will wait until we get there to make ours. I will get there before Kaurin and begin house hunting.

I really should be cleaning house but as I have already cleaned one this summer all my ambition seems to be used up.

All my sewing is done. I even finished my comforter cover. My dresses all turned out quite well. I made nine all together. I hope to get to Seattle with at least one clean. The boys' things are all ready too.

Will close. Victor has just brought me a dandelion bouquet and must have a glass to put it in.

Hope you are all well. Love to all from all,

Marion

St. Michael, Alaska
July 7, 1936

Dear Mother,

Was glad to get your letter and all the news it contained. I have been here for a month now and will be here until about the 20th of September. The July boat will be here around the middle of the month but we are staying until the boat after that. At first we planned to leave here in the summer but we have enough groceries and fuel to last nearly all summer so there would have been no advantage in leaving so soon. Also, I don't like hot weather, though it has been very hot here. The boys went around in nothing but shirts and overalls. It is raining right now but the weather has been unusually good and warm since the middle of April. We will probably have an awful fall to get even. Maybe the weatherman is making me a going away present.

I am supposed to be on vacation but I don't get one from medical work. The Eskimos here are after me all the time. One of the boys from Stebbins came over here for the 4th of July and broke his leg. They came for me and I put splints on. Then I wired for the *Northland*, the revenue cutter, as there is a doctor on her. She was at Shaktoolik so got here yesterday noon. The doctor was two hours setting the bones and putting on a cast. It was a bad break and he won't be able to walk before Christmas. Then we visited all the sick while the doctor was here.

It seems good not to have to do much but keep house. I certainly enjoyed the first week over here. There were several people here and we just had a good time. We ate at all hours and went to bed when we got tired. We were up all night one night and most of the next as we were expecting the *Vic* any minute.

Kaurin is up the river now. He will be gone a long time on this trip as they have about three hundred tons of freight to deliver going up and another three hundred on the return trip. They also have to make a side trip to bring in two hundred tons of salt salmon. Want some? The last freighter that was here delivered eight hundred tons of freight, the most that has been delivered at one time in fourteen years.

Kaurin connected some oil tanks and ran a pipe into the kitchen so that I don't have to go out of doors to get water. It is quite an improvement. All the women envy me. It is raining enough so that the tanks are full all the time, no matter how much I use. It is really great.

The boys were pleased with their cards. Francis was going to write but is never in the house except to eat and sleep. I am afraid he won't like living in the city so well if he has to stay in his own yard. Life in the States will be a great change in most ways.

Lovingly, Marion

On Board *S.S. McKinley*
October 6, 1936

Dear Mother,
Tomorrow night at this time we should be in Seattle although we may get in too late to dock and have to spend another night on board. We have been on board since the 22nd of September. The sailing from Seattle was delayed and the ship made so many stops coming up that we were very much later in leaving Alaska than we expected to be.

We are on a new ship on this run. She is larger and much better appointed than the old *Victoria*, also more expensive to travel on. We have a very nice room, two single beds, a pullman berth, bench chair, clothes closet, four large drawers and running hot and cold water. The closet door is a mirror so that you can get a full view.

It has been quite a rough trip but we were not very sick. Victor was the worst. He has eaten almost nothing the whole trip. I missed two meals but it was mostly because it was so rough a couple of nights that I couldn't sleep and was too tired to get up. The meals have been good but some people complain a lot. Tomorrow night will be the captain's dinner and we are looking forward to that.

Kaurin is still in St. Michael. He expected to come out on the *Vic*'s last trip but she is all sold out so I guess he is going to have to fly to Anchorage and then come by boat from there. That means he won't be out until about Thanksgiving.

We are all well. I am beginning to feel the change in temperature already. It had snowed some before we left St. Michael and although it was quite warm when we left, it is much warmer down here.

We have been having a hard time getting up these mornings. For the past six nights the clocks have been advanced half an hour each night.

We have been making good time since leaving the Aleutians, over 300 sea miles a day. A strong wind is blowing and the ship is heeled over like a sailing ship.

There are about two hundred passengers on board but about one hundred of them are steerage passengers so we don't see many people. There is an orchestra on board. They play for meals and up in the club room when it is calm enough. There is a bar in the club room and everyone smokes so I don't go up. There are four decks on this boat. The *Vic* has only two. The *McKinley*, under another name, used to sail in the Caribbean. She was built in 1918.

My address in Seattle will be the Claremont Hotel, Fourth and Virginia, for a time. I will write you again as soon as we are settled. Kaurin wants me to go house hunting. That will be new for me and I haven't the least idea how to go about it. I don't know what I should look for. We do plan to buy though. I'm sure I'll be able to find someone to help me.

P. S. Our farewell at St. Michael was not easy. After sixteen years in the area our roots were pretty deep. It was sad to say goodbye to our old friends for the last time.

Lots of love,

Marion

Seattle, Washington, U.S.A.
November 6, 1936

Dear Mother,

At last we know where we are going to live. We have bought a house on Vashon Island. It is really out in the country as there are woods on one side of the house. We have about an acre of ground, enough to have a nice garden. The house is not large, only five rooms and bath; no basement but an attic without a stairway. Also, the roof needs reshingling. But we have lots of big windows and it is a very bright and sunny looking house.

I must buy some dishes and cooking utensils but I get cold feet every time I go looking for anything. The prices seem so high! We paid $1,800 for the house and that made an awful hole in our bank account.

Kaurin got here just three weeks after we did. He managed to get on the *Vic* after all but he says it was very crowded.

We have bought bedroom furniture and a stove for the kitchen. I will be burning wood. My range in St. Michael was green and cream so this time we got an ivory color and I am going to buy ivory and red cooking dishes. We are enjoying all this so much, especially our trees on the island. Some different than St. Michael.

Seems wonderful to have the four of us together again. We are surely going to enjoy our new home.

Write when you can,

Marion and Family

EPILOGUE

Seattle, Washington
June 11, 1979

Dear Don,

Thank you for your nice letter. It was good to hear from you again. I will try to answer your questions in the order in which you asked them.

Kaurin died of a heart attack in Unalakleet in 1947 while on his way home from a summer's work on the Yukon. He never lost his love for the sea and each shipping season headed north to run the rivers again. He was buried in St. Michael next to the grave of Baby Kaurin.

The Fred of the letters died some years ago but Tom settled here in Seattle. I caught a glimpse of him on a crowded bus one day but he got off before I could reach him.

As to the reason for the long intervals between some of the letters, a good share of the time I did not have the two cents to mail a letter. I think it was those years that have made me the careful soul I am today. How we ever kept out of debt I'll never understand.

The two babies came along in that period too. Francis cost $110 and Baby Kaurin $100. That doesn't seem like so much now but it was pretty bad at that time and there was no welfare to turn to for help. I remember earning $15 on the first bill by embroidering some curtains.

Yes, Don, I did drive the dog teams occasionally but never alone. Our dogs were too wild and eager to go. Sometimes Kaurin would ski ahead of them and I would drive. One time we were taking movies of them and I drove out with the kids on the sled. When we got back Francis wanted to know how Mom looked driving and his dad told him, "Just like a big black moose going down the trail." Not very flattering but l expect my old black fur coat was standing out behind.

I am now remarried to Walter Gregerson and we make our home in Seattle.

I must close now but would like to say one last word about Alaska. I do have a great admiration for the older generation of Eskimos. They were a happy, hard working, honest people. I enjoyed my years with them and feel that our time there was rewarding and fulfilling.

Best wishes to you and yours,

Marion

Grand Rapids, Michigan
March 20, 1992

Dear Don,

   I was delighted to receive your recent letter. I will try to answer your questions concerning Marion and her family.

   Marion has moved from Seattle and is now living in Anacortes, Washington. Her vision is failing but she gets around fairly well in spite of that handicap. It bothers her not to be able to read and do the things she likes to. She was always so active and up and doing.

   Marion, our brother Leonard and I are each alone now.   Walter Gregerson passed away last summer. Leonard is on a trip. In the summer he has a part time job. Not bad for a man of 85.

   Marion's son Victor passed away February 22, 1979 in Anacortes. Her other son, Frances, lives just six miles away and checks on her every day. He is a very devoted son and one to be proud of.

   Hope you are enjoying your winter in Florida. It seems to be a favorite spot for the Michigan natives; they are either going to or coming from there.

   Love,

                                                    Helen